How to Do Precision Self Therapy to Quickly Change Anything in your Life

Book 1 of 3

The Psycanics Life Transformation System

Mycal Powell

How to Do Precision Self Therapy
To Quickly Change Anything In Your Life

Published by **Essentiality Press,** a division of the
Psycanics Science Institute, Inc. 501c3,

Los Angeles, California, USA.
Xalapa, Veracruz, México

ISBN   978-0-9981594-4-7

Library of Congress Control Number: No

Subjects and keywords

Self-Help   Self-Therapy

Personal Development   Personal Growth   Transformation

Psychology Psychotherapy

Philosophy   Ontology

Spirituality, Awakening, Enlightenment, Illumination

Spiritual Development, Spiritual Self-Help

Acknowledgements and Gratitude:

Alline Powell, executive officer for ThEO:
The Enlightenment Organization,
and a master of Psycanics and piloting in her own right.

Issis León, my personal BTT pilot and spiritual channel of many years.

Angel González, former student and now a master in his own right.

My many enlightened students who have
taught me as much as I them.

Value

The knowledge in this book is the result of 40 years of investigation of the ultimate nature of existence at a cost of more than $5,000,000 USD. It is yours for the price of the books.

Responsability

How you use this knowledge and your results are purely your responsability. There is no known danger to it except that, very rarely, a person may activate an emotional charge that he needs piloting help to discreate. The Psycanics Science Institute is always here to help.

Table of Contents

1- The Promise of this Book

Introduction to
The Psycanics Life Transformation System and
its Being Transformation Technology

How To Do Precision Self-Therapy
To Quickly Change Anything in Your Life.

How to Achieve True Happiness

All The Time, No Matter What.

This book is for those who want to know precisely, scientifically, how their life really works so they can take control of theirs and create the life they want.

The Purpose and Promise of this book:

The purpose of this book is to show you how to control your life, eliminate all negatives, and manifest in each of the 6 Arenas of your life the positive things you wish to experience. The objective is to achieve True Happiness which is living in positive results and emotions (satisfaction, enthusiasm, love, joy, etc.) all the time, no matter what. (See our free course on True Happiness and how to achieve it.) This takes about 400 hours of work on your Self, which most students accomplish in about 2 years. Here is how it works:

Life consists of 6 Arenas of experience, which form the

Causal Sequence of the Six Arenas in which life occurs:

BE → FEEL → THINK → RELATE & DO → HAVE

These are equivalent to:

Identities → Emotions → Mind → Behaviors & Actions → Results

It is a Causal Sequence: each element to the left determines
the elements to the right.

The initial and ONLY fully causal element of all the 6 Arenas is your BEing.
You, the BEing, are the only thing alive, the only thing with power to decide,
act, create, and manifest in your life
(which consists of many Causal Sequences).
All the other Arenas are results, products, of your BEing.

Life is simple:

➢ Positive states of BEing naturally produce positive results and satisfaction (happiness) across all the other 5 Arenas of life.

➢ Negative states of BEing cannot but produce negative results and pain across all the other Arenas of life.

Control your BEing by discreating your negative IDentities and creating positive ones, and you can control will minimal additional effort all the rest of your life.

This book explains what BEing and IDentities are and how to create and discreate them.

Just as a trim tab of only 3 square feet can control a 747 airliner of 1 million pounds, so too can you control your life with a little effort focused on your exact and true point of power: your BEing.

The Quantum Revolution in Psychology that is Psycanics

This book presents a revolution in the understanding of human psychology and behavior. It is not an advancement or evolution of psychology today; it is totally new paradigm, a quantum leap to a new level of knowledge, like the shifts from the old belief that the Earth is flat to knowing it is a sphere, and from the sun revolving around to the Earth, to knowing the Earth revolves around the sun. **Psycanics is as far advanced beyond psychology today as quantum physics is beyond Newtonian mechanics.**

From the theory comes the Psycanics Being Transformation Technology (BTT). It is a system of personal change, of "psycho-therapy". It is precise, powerful, fast, certain, universal, and easier to learn and apply than all current psycho-therapies. BTT (Being Transformation Technology) not only serves to remedy any particular aberration that the client desires, but also to eliminate all negative emotions (anger, fear, sadness, guilt, hate, depression, etc.) and to transform his entire life into all positive experiences and behaviors.

Let us clarify the title of this book: **How To Do Precision Self-Therapy To Quickly Change Anything in Your Life.**

By "self-therapy", we mean you will learn:

1- How to find within yourself, in your mind or subconscious, the underlying, TRUE CAUSE of any negative feeling or behavior you wish to change.

2- How to eliminate that causal element from your being; how to "dis-create" it. (To discreate something is to cause that it no longer exists.)

3- How to create whatever positive experience or behavior you desire.

4- If you continue to practice the self-therapy technology in this book, you can eliminate ALL your negative emotions and behaviors.

Our objective is that you learn to do the procedure on yourself; that you do not need another person (a therapist). You will then be able to repeat it on all your negative emotions. It only takes an hour or two to eliminate any particular *trigger-negative-emotion* combo. It takes about 400 hours of work on yourself to eliminate all your negative emotions and behaviors. Most people achieve that in about two years. This state of zero negative emotions is essential to True Happiness as we explain below.

By "Anything"

All your negative experiences and negative behaviors occur in one of the Six Arenas of Life: **BE, FEEL, THINK, RELATE & DO, HAVE.** BTT works to change anything in any of the Arenas, which we introduce here:

HAVE: You will be able to transform negative personal situations such as relationships, work or business, and financial status, and ease any health problems caused by repressed emotions. You will be able to transform your relationships to harmony, love, and cooperation. You will know how to manifest the money and the experiences (such as travel and vacations) that you desire.

DO: You will be able to discreate your negative behaviors such as compulsions, obsessions, addictions to any substance or activity (e.g.: tobacco, alcohol, drugs; gambling, sex/porn). You will also be able to discreate irresponsibility, laziness, and aversions to others. You will be able to discreate all fear and phobias to taking action: for examples: fear of flying, writer's block, changing jobs, starting a business, timidity, fear of speaking in public, marrying/divorcing, etc.

RELATE: You will know how to eliminate the root causes of problems and conflicts in your relationships.

THINK: You will know how to erase all negative energy from your mind. You will be able to discreate painful memories, traumatic incidents including PTSD, and all the psychological effects of abandonment, violence, abuse, rape, etc., whether recent or in your childhood. You will remove the compulsion to invalidate, judge, and criticize others; and the compulsion to control or manipulate them. (These are a major cause of problems and conflicts in relationships.)

FEEL: You will be able to discreate permanently ALL your negative emotions: anger, fear, guilt, sorrow, resentment, hate, grief, depression, etc.

BE: And the most important of all: you will understand what you are, what you being is and know how re-create it in your highest ideal of who you want to BE. Your BEing is the most powerful factor in shaping your experience and your life. Most of it is subconscious. You will learn to find the elements of your BEing that are causing your negative results in life, discreate them, and then re-create yourself in your highest ideal of who you want to be.

Aberrations

An aberration is any deviation in your life, in your experience, from what you desire. Negative emotions, behaviors, thoughts, relationships with problems and conflicts are all aberrations from what (we assume) you desire in your life experience: results and happiness. Here is a partial list of all the aberrations that psycanics can eliminate.

Partial List of Aberrations that Psycanics Eliminates:

Emotions: You can permanently eliminate all the negative emotions: anger, anxiety, fear, guilt, resentment, hate, sorrow, grief, loneliness, including

- **phobias** (heights, flying, water, snakes, dying, rats: whatever).
- **depression** (I discreated my own suicidal depression in 2001), and
- **existential stress and crises** (about such things as divorce, losing job, cancer, death of a loved one, fear of death, etc.)
- **PTSD**. Eliminating any PTSD only takes a few hours of BTT.

Identity: You can eliminate all experiences of **negative identity, self-image and self-esteems. Examples:** I am less intelligent than others; I can't do it; I am unable; I am a failure; I am not good enough; I am less than others; I am undeserving; I am unworthy; I am bad; etc. One of the major reasons you cannot produce what you want in life is the Law of Power that: **You cannot manifest anything in your physical universe that would contradict Who You Are (the sum of your identities)**.

Self-image and self-esteem: Many behavioral problems stem from negative self-image and the negative self-esteem that results. Being Transformation Technology (BTT) guides the explorer to the negative states of BEing that produce negative self-image-esteem so that the client can discreate them and re-create himself in positive identities.

> **Definition: Explorer:** a person who is exploring his psycanic universe and making changes by discreating negative realities and creating positive ones using the Being Transformation Technology (explained in this book).

> **Definition: Pilot:** a person highly trained in psycanics and Being Transformation Technology, able to guide others in their explorations, creations and discreations. While the objective is for all explorers to learn to do their own therapy, pilots are invaluable for training and for complicated charges beyond the experience level of (new) explorers.

Note: Identities and mental realities cannot be changed by merely "changing your mind". Nor can you plaster over them with positive realities (such as affirmations). The Law is: *You cannot create positive over the top of negative already present in your BEing.* All negative experiences and behaviors are causes by realities, by masses of energy in your subconscious. These must be **discreated**. Gone the negative reality, the positive manifests with only minimal energization.

Mind: You can eliminate all negative thoughts and limiting beliefs. Examples of limiting beliefs: "Money is scarce." "You have to work hard to have money." "Only corrupt/bad people have money" which is followed unconsciously by

"As I don't want to be bad, I will not have money." All men are _____. "
"All women are _____. "Life is hard." "People are out to get me"; etc.

Behaviors: eliminate or change any negative behavior:

- laziness, irresponsibility, impunctuality.

- blocks to taking action (for example: writer's block, to leaving a job, to starting a business, to getting a divorce, stage fright, performance anxiety, anorexia nervosa (block to eating), shyness, etc.).

- **addictions** to substances: (e.g. alcohol, tobacco, prescription meds, illegal drugs, etc.) The negative energy structures in the human Shell that produce addictions are the same for all addictions.

- all **compulsions** to negative activities (e.g. gambling, porn, sex, retail therapy (over shopping), overeating, social media, video and computer games, etc.)

- all **attachments** (a person has an attachment if the loss of any person or thing would produce UPS).

Traumatic incidents:

You will be able to erase all the trauma from events, both from the past (often childhood) and in the present. Examples of traumatic incidents include violence, rape, abandonment, abuse, death of a loved one, accidents, severe illnesses (e.g. cancer), divorce, etc.

> Note: BTT eliminates the emotional charges and behavioral compulsions, turning a traumatic incident into a simple, matter-of-fact memory. It does not erase the memory of the event.

PTSD: Psycanics cures PTSD quickly, in a few hours of BTT processing.

Relationships: BTT identifies the root causes of almost all relationship problems and conflicts. Once the person has discreated those, his relationships transform to harmony, love, and cooperation. Only one of the parties needs to discreate his negative relationship energies; when one person changes, the other changes naturally.

The body and physical health: Many health problems are caused by negative energy --usually emotions such as anger, resentment, hate, fear, guilt, grief, etc. -- repressed into the body. Psycanics will guide you to find and discharge that energy and create healing and health in that area. This usually produces an improvement in the area and sometimes cures the problem completely.

By "Precision"

We mean that the procedure to identify and eliminate the causes of negative energy in your life and install your desired positive results is exact; it is surgical; it is laser-like. It is "Step 1, Step 2, Step 3, etc.". There is nothing hazy, uncertain, fuzzy, or trial-and-error about the Psycanics Being Transformation Technology or its results of transforming your BEing and life. This book gives you exact laws and formula, and a schematic, of how your life _really_ works. The science behind this book, psycanics, is a quantum leap in psychology and psychotherapy.

By "Quickly"

We mean that you will be able to change some things in as little as an hour of your application of the technology in this book. Most experiences and behaviors you will be able to transform in 2 to 5 hours. Even traumas and PTSD only take a few hours. About 400 hours (which you can do over a few years) is enough to permanently eliminate all your negative emotions and behaviors so that you live in serenity, peace and joy all the time.

True Happiness

True happiness is living in a state of positive emotions **all the time no matter what.** A person who is Truly Happy resides in the upper half of the **Happiness<>UPS Polarity Spectrum** (illustrated below). (UPS is the acronym for Unhappiness, Pain, and Suffering). He rarely ever descends into the lower half of the Spectrum, the negative emotions. If he does, he knows how to quickly and permanently discreate that negative emotion.

If you are living with frequent activations of your negative emotions (anger, anxiety, fear, guilt, sadness, loneliness, hate, depression, etc.), you do not qualify as happy. You are not "steady state" happy; you are alternating back and forth between emotional pain (unhappiness) and positive emotions (happiness). That is not True Happiness.

Here is an analogy to understand this: If you are healthy one day but the next are sick; but then healthy again; but then in the hospital and then out and then in again; and so live alternating between healthy and ill, day to day or even hour to hour; **you are not healthy**. To qualify as "healthy", you must be free of illness for long periods, better yet, always.

In the same way, if you are bouncing up and down between positive and negative emotions in your life; you do not qualify as Happy. If you are content one moment, then angry, then excited, then anxious, then enthusiastic, but then feeling guilt or sorrow, or depression, you are not living True Happiness. You are on the emotional roller coaster, alternating up and down, between positive and negative emotions, between feeling good and emotional pain. You are playing emotional basketball, bouncing up and down, "vibrating" between fleeting moments of pleasure and of pain. Your positive moments are soon marred, damaged, destroyed, by your negative emotions. That is a life of way too much Unhappiness, Pain and Suffering (UPS)* to be considered happy.

Illustration: The Happiness<>UPS Polarity Spectrum. Happiness is living in positive emotions all the time, no matter what. You qualify as Happy when you live completely in the upper half of the Spectrum, free of all the negative emotions in the lower half. Happiness is very rare among ordinary humans for reasons we shall see in this book. However, it is atainable by anyone who makes the effort – it takes two to four years of BTT.

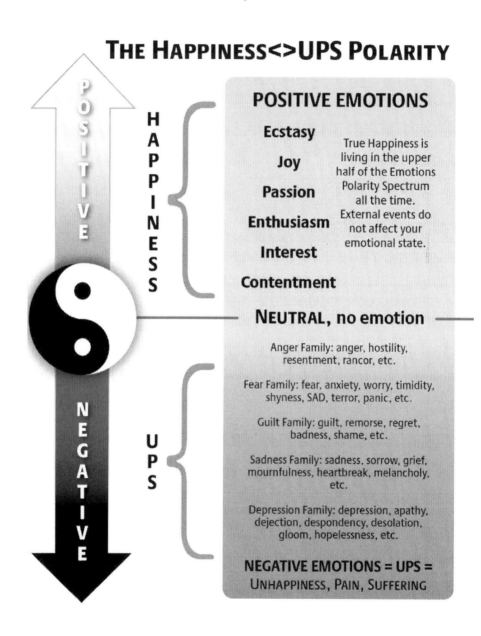

THE HAPPINESS<>UPS POLARITY

POSITIVE EMOTIONS

Ecstasy

Joy

Passion

Enthusiasm

Interest

Contentment

True Happiness is living in the upper half of the Emotions Polarity Spectrum all the time. External events do not affect your emotional state.

NEUTRAL, no emotion

Anger Family: anger, hostility, resentment, rancor, etc.

Fear Family: fear, anxiety, worry, timidity, shyness, SAD, terror, panic, etc.

Guilt Family: guilt, remorse, regret, badness, shame, etc.

Sadness Family: sadness, sorrow, grief, mournfulness, heartbreak, melancholy, etc.

Depression Family: depression, apathy, dejection, despondency, desolation, gloom, hopelessness, etc.

NEGATIVE EMOTIONS = UPS =
UNHAPPINESS, PAIN, SUFFERING

*Definition: **UPS**: abbreviation for **Unhappiness, Pain, and Suffering**, always referring to your psycanic (mental and emotional) experience unless "physical" pain or suffering is specified.) Your own negative emotions are the only UPS that you know.

Thus, the first and essential step to your True Happiness is to eliminate ALL your negative emotions. This book shows you how to do so. This book is not only about how to eliminate any particular negative experience or behavior, but how to eliminate ALL of them. This takes about 400 hours of the Psycanics' Being Transformation Technology (BTT) which most students achieve within two years. I can speak to you of this with authority because I and all the graduates of the Psycanics Science Institute have achieved the elimination of our negative emotions.

Recommended *The Psycanics True Happiness Course* videos on YouTube or at www.Psyanics.org.

Two Illustrations next page: We reduce the full-page Spectrum of Happiness<>UPS above to one half size and place two contrasting graphs: top and bottom.

Top: **NOT HAPPINESS**:   The ordinary human being lives bouncing between positive and negative experience (in mind and emotions), and with many negative behaviors (e.g. addictions, neuroses, relationship problems, etc.). He is frequently activated in negative emotions = emotional pain and suffering (UPS). He lives with mediocre results and his life is full of Drama (TT).

Bottom: **TRUE HAPPINESS**: The wise, powerful and Truly Happy person has *permanently* discreated all his negative emotions and behaviors. He then lives in positive emotions and behaviors all the time (True Happiness), and easily produces his desired results in his relationships and manifests what he wants in the physical universe.

The ordinary human being lives bouncing between positive and negative emotions. Has lots of negative behaviors. Life is full of pain; does not qualify as Happy.

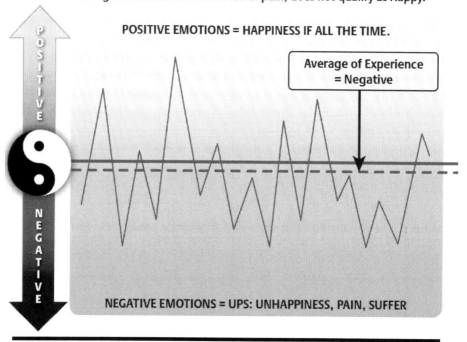

The Truly Happy person has eliminated all negative emotions and behaviors, and lives in positive emotions all the time, no matter what happens to him.

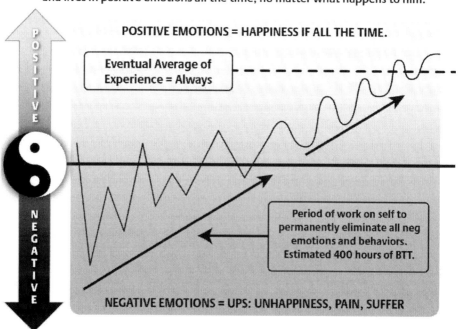

2- The Source of This Knowledge

Essentiality and Psycanics

You are entering into the study of a new and revolutionary science of BEing and life called psycanics, which itself is a trickle-down from an even more advanced body of knowledge: Essentiality. Together, these two explain, with concise laws and formulas, **who you are, what you are doing on Earth, and how your life and happiness really work**. These new sciences are at the cutting edge of human knowledge, beyond all psychology and philosophy on the planet until now, and in fact combine them and spirituality into one system of knowledge.

Essence

The highest source of the knowledge in this book is a system of spirituality called Essentiality. Essentiality is a scientific model of the nature of Essence. Everything exists is One Infinite BEing, which we shall call Essence because She is the essence of all that is. She is the only thing that truly exists; the Creation is an illusion. She creates everything in the Creation out of Her Self, out of Her divine Essence Energy. She is both the Creator and the Creation. She has 13 Primordial Characteristics: Oneness/Unity, Infinity, Light, Consciousness, Wisdom, Will (Power), Perfection, Beauty, Magnificence, Love, Peace, Joy, and Truth.

How do we know all this? We, the publishers of this book, are mystics and have achieved the level of consciousness know in Buddhism as enlightenment. We are enlightened BEings. This means that we have transcended the illusion of being a human being and recovered our moment-to-moment experience of ourselves as immortal spiritual BEings just visiting Earth to enjoy the Human Adventure Movie. We regularly travel in consciousness outside of the physical universe, both into the depths of our own BEing and into higher dimensions of the Infinite Creation. We can perceive, feel, and communicate with the Creator, i.e. God, the Infinite BEing of Love we call Essence.

There is nothing special about us; any person willing to make the effort can do all that we have done. **We are all equal BEings, children of Essence.** Essence is all around you all the time; She is inside you; everything is Essence taking the form. The great question is: Why do you not perceive Her? In our advanced materials, Essentiality, we answer that question and teach those who wish to know how to do so. In our basic materials, Psycanics, to which this book is an introduction, we teach you how to transform your human life.

Be clear that nothing we say has anything to do with religion. There is no dogma, belief or faith involved. You will be able to understand all that we say and you will be able to verify it all in your own experience.

You, Psycan

You are a spirit, an individualization of the One Infinite BEing, of Essence. You are a non-physical, life-energy entity of aware-will, called a psycan. You-psycan are spiritual being visiting Earth and pretending to be human in order to live your personal Human Adventure Movie. Your divine and original nature is Essence, is the 13 Characteristics – which you must block out to play the Human Game.

The importance of this is that, for you to take power over your being and life, it greatly helps to understand who and what you are. As a "child of Essence" you are a creator; you are the creator of all your experience and your life. You are currently creating unconsciously and many negative things. We are going to show you how you are doing so and how to change to creating consciously and the positive things you want.

The Creation

The Creation consists of an infinity of dimensions and universes (Cap "C" when referring to the entire Creation.) The purpose of the Creation is EXPERIENCE, every kind of experience possible without exception or limitation. Essence expresses and manifests Her Self as the Creation to explore and experience in all Her infinite possibilities of BE, DO, HAVE.

Movie Theaters

Each world in each universe is like a movie theater. We-spirits (psycans) incarnate on a world in order to live its movie. You are currently incarnated on Earth to live your Human Movie, which is mostly about the exploration of Drama (TT). To live your Human Movie, you must block out Who You Really Are (spirit child of Essence) and fully immerse yourself, lose your Self, in your human role. You do the same when, as a human being, you go to your local theater to watch a movie. You forget who you are, identify with the hero, lose yourself in the plot, all to savor the drama of the movie. Only by forgetting who you really are outside of the theater can you lose yourself in the movie's illusion and maximally enjoy it. This is exactly what you-psycan are doing here on Earth: starring in your Human Movie.

The Matrix

The Matrix is a famous, 1999 movie about how our world is an illusion created by the "evil machines" to suck human energy for their purposes. In the movie, we humans are living inside the Matrix (this world) totally oblivious to its true nature and function. A few humans wake up by taking the Red Pill and realize what is going on and begin to fight against the machines.

This is the truth! Our world is literally a Matrix. It is a perfectly-real illusion, a theater, where we-psycans (spirit incarnations of Essence) come to play, to experience. There an infinity of Matrices (worlds) in the Creation; ours is the Human Adventure. The great difference is that in our real Matrix of the Human World, outside is not the "evil machines" but Essence, the Creator of Infinite Love-Joy. You are a spark of God playing in the Creation.

YOU ARE IN THE MATRIX.

You are **asleep** in the Matrix living your Dream of being human.
You will be here for as many incarnations/lifetimes as you please and
until you AWAKEN to Who You Really Are and reconnect to Essence.

Although this book is about you achieving True Happiness,
the same technology begins Awakening.

Human Incarnations

A complete cycle of the exploration of the Human Experience comprises hundreds of incarnations. You explore as many possibilities of the Human Experience as possible: male<> female<>homosexual, rich<> poor, warrior<> priest, nun<> prostitute, success<> failure, healthy<> sick, famous<> nobody, black<> white<>all colors, tyrant<> oppressed, die young<> die old, etc. I realize that many people believe that there is no such thing as re-incarnation. However, I have processed hundreds of past lives, my own and those of my students. If you give me a roomful of people, I can put many in touch with a past life within 10 minutes using the Being Transformation Technology introduced in this book. If you apply the technology in this book, you will eventually encounter your own past lives. They are only important where they contain energy charges that are affecting you in this lifetime and so need to be cleaned with BTT.

How do I know all this? I and dozens of people in the Essentiality School of Accelerated Enlightenment have awakened and reached enlightenment. We live in this realities and experience all the time.

Awakening and Enlightenment

Knowledge is Power: this book has knowledge with which you can change anything in your life or transform it entirely. You can:

1. Change a particular negative experience, behavior, or relationship problem in your life (Level #1). And that is fine: this book will do that. But it is like using 16-inch naval battleship guns to sink a rowboat. This book is far more powerful than just changing something in your life; it is the portal to higher levels of personal and spiritual development including

2. Eliminate ALL your negative emotions and behaviors and create a life of True Happiness, of wisdom, power, love and abundance.

3. Begin your spiritual Awakening within the Matrix and achieve Enlightenment. You then live as a spirit (psycan) free of your human identity illusion and of all Drama and UPS, and consciously manifests what he wishes to experience.

4. Go beyond Enlightenment, its full spiritual Illumination, the state of Buddha and Jesus, in which you transcend all illusion of individuality and separation from the One and return to BEing the One, God, again.

How far you go is up to you.

When you-spirit-psycan tire of the Human Game, you can awaken and recover your awareness of Who You Really Are, a psycan formed of Essence and connected to the One (as we all are). This awakening is the core teaching of all religions. Essentiality is a science –*not a religion*- of how to awaken and so reach spiritual enlightenment. I am such a being; I have awakened from the Human Dream and now live, not as a human being, but as an immortal spirit, a psycan, visiting Earth and operating a human body. I have hundreds of times traveled outside of the physical universe (FU) visiting both the inner dimensions of my own BEing and other dimensions of the Creation including communing with Essence. That is how I can write all that is in this book: I am passing on to you Her teachings. Nor am I a fluke; all the advanced students of the Essentiality School of Accelerated Enlightenment are enlightened and have similar experiences; and we are here to serve others in achieving all this for themselves. Nor are any of us special cases: what we have done is possible to all. We are all equal spirits, individualizations of Essence.

All the above is *verifiable* in personal experience by anyone willing to follow instructions and make the effort. No belief or faith required. Students begin to be able to experience Essence themselves in their third or fourth year of study in the Essentiality School of Accelerated Enlightenment.

Spirituality versus Religion. Do not confuse these two words.

➢ Spirituality refers to the nature of spirit, of nonphysical, life-energy entities, such as your Self. You are an immortal spirit, an individualization of the One Great Spirit, Creator and Essence of all that is. Your spirituality is a question of your experience of Who You Really Are and your actions expressing that, especially how you treat others: with positive energy or negative energy, with love or anti-love. Your spirituality is also your degree of experience and expression of the One Great Spirit, Essence. Jesus and Buddha are famous for achieving a high level of the experience and expression of Essence.

➢ A religion is a name-brand collection of dogmas and doctrines about god or gods. A religion is a mental substitution of beliefs and faith for personal experience. If there were any real experience, any true knowledge, in a religion; there would be no need for belief and faith.

There is nothing religious in this book: no dogmas and psycanics never asks for belief or faith. This book is highly spiritual, because YOU are immortal spirit entity of aware-will incarnating on Earth to star in your Human Adventure Movies. It also introduces the Great Infinite Spirit, Creator and Essence of all things and from whom you come. You cannot truly understand human nature and your own BEing without understanding your spirit-uality and your true Essence.

Nothing in psycanics or Essentiality is "religious", no belief involved, because you can verify all that we say in your own experience. It takes about 4 years of 1 hour of BTT per day to be able to perceive and communicate with Essence. This is much less time and effort than it would take you to verify the advanced phenomena in physical science such as black holes, quasars, quarks, or the Higgs boson.

Psycanics

Out of Essentiality comes Psycanics. It is the science of your non-physical energies, of your trans-physical experience. Your trans-physical energies-experiences include all your emotions, positive and negative; all your thoughts and mental activities; your identities and self-image, your communications and relationship energies, love, and your happiness or suffering in life.

All your non-physical experiences (mind, emotions, identities, etc.) are energies you-psycan perceive, but they are not physical. They do not come from the physical universe; you do not perceive them through your body, but directly in your consciousness, in your BEing which is aware-will. We call all of these your **psycanic** energies, your **psycanic** experience (to distinguish them from your physical experiences). Your psycanic energies cause your interior, private life.

In summary:

➢ **Essentiality** deals with the nature of Essence (the Creator, God), your true spiritual nature as an individualization of Essence, as a psycan; and with your perception, relationship, and communication with Essence, i.e. God.

➢ **Psycanics** deals with your creation and control of your human life. It presents the laws of your internal experience (identities, emotions, thoughts), your relationships, love, happiness; and your ability to manifest what you want in your external, physical universe.

Here is the breakthrough in psychology that is Psycanics: everything in your internal, psycanic world operates just as does everything in your external, physical world: **according to exact laws and principles.**

The laws that determine:
- ✓ what you feel,
- ✓ what you think,
- ✓ how you behave,
- ✓ the quality and harmony of your relationships,
- ✓ your ability to manifest in the FU (FU = physical universe) what you want (success and abundance, etc.)
- ✓ and therefore, your happiness or unhappiness . . .

. . . are just as precise and powerful as the laws that hold the planets in their orbits.

Everything in your mind and emotions and behaviors is "legal"; everything functions according to the laws of psycanic energy. These laws are similar to, but not exactly the same as, the laws of physical energy. There is nothing random or accidental in your internal, psycanic world -- and it is all under your control when you understand the laws and principles of psycanic energy. Where your life is chaotic, it is because you do not understand how it works and so create chaos.

You will be learning some of these laws in this book: they will give you power and control over your interior, psycanic universe, just as the laws of physics have given mankind control over the physical universe. You will be able to transform your internal world from jungle to garden.

Psycanics is 10 times more precise and faster than all current psychologies in producing personal change and development. Furthermore, each person can learn to apply it to himself and so be able to change everything he wants in his life, to re-create and transform his life as he would have it. Few people have the time or the money to run to a therapist every time they want to eliminate a negative emotion or behavior.

Jungle to Garden

The ordinary human being lives in a psycanic jungle. A jungle is full of wild plants, spiderwebs, thorns and minds, so thick it is hard to even push through. In the same way, the inner experience of the ordinary human being is a jungle full of negative emotions (anger, anxiety, fear, guilt, sadness, aversions, hate, depression, etc.), negative thoughts, negative self-image-esteem, and relationship frustrations. All these energies are activation and jumping around in his experience like popcorn going off in a hot cooker.

Psycanics empowers you to weed out all your negative energies and then plant the positive ones that you want to experience. It is like weeding out a dense, dark jungle and then planting fruit trees and flowers to create a garden. Your interior life then unfolds as the Garden of Eden instead of the valley of darkness and tears.

3- Magic

**Any sufficiently advanced technology
is indistinguishable from magic.**
Arthur C. Clarke

Imagine going back in time and showing a television, a cell phone, or a jet plane to people 1000 years ago. What would they think on seeing the dancing figures of a movie on a TV screen? What would they think to see you talking to someone on your computer screen (e.g. Skype or Zoom), or on your cell phone and hear them respond? What would they feel to see an airliner take off? What would they feel if they were on an airliner taking off? What would they think on seeing a medical operation?

On having no idea of modern science and technology, they could only stand in awe of the magic, the wizardry, the miracle. Our machines today are complex and powerful beyond their imagination, beyond their powers of comprehension. To those who don't know, science and technology are magic.

Not Evolution but a Quantum Leap

A quantum jump in physics is an instantaneous change from one state to another with no intervening progression, movement. For tens of thousands of years, the "knowledge" of humanity about how existence works was superstitions and myths. (These are a tribute to the power of the human mind to create realities, to hallucinate explanations.) Modern science began with the Renaissance about 1300 and took off with Newtonian (classical) physics and calculus in the 1600's. Modern physics (includes relativity, quantum mechanics, and astrophysics) began about 1900. You enjoy the fruits of quantum physics every day: your cellphone depends on it. You use relativity frequently: GPS must take it into account to give you your location.

The progress of knowledge from superstition to Newtonian physics to quantum mechanics is not linear; it is not a smooth development or evolution from one to the other. Each physics is a quantum leap from the previous system of thought to the new one. In fact, one of the barriers to the adoption of the new system was the necessity to throw off the previous, to exit the old paradigm.

In the same way, psycanics is not a progression, an evolution, of psychology and psycho-therapy. It deals with the same phenomena, human experience and behavior, but with a radically new paradigm. Psycanics is much more similar to physics and electronics than it is to psychology. Psycanics deals with cause⬦effect, force, power, energy, mass, realities, energy flow, resistances, energy discharge, creation and discreation. It deals with you as a spirit, a life-energy entity of aware-will, with the power to move energy, and so create and discreate realities. So please take notice that in studying psycanics, you are making a quantum leap to a new science about how life works. Anything that you know from psychology will be more a hindrance than a help.

Power

The scientific word for magic is power. **Power is the ability to produce the desired results.** All our modern technology is power: factories, automobiles, computers, internet, cellphones, medicine, etc. Where does our power come from? From knowledge, from science which is systematic knowledge. How much knowledge does it take to produce and maintain operating our civilization? Universities, millions of books, years of study and specialization: there is so much to know that no one person can know more than a small piece of the entire puzzle of our civilization.

We are promising you magical levels of power over your life, over your mind, emotions, behaviors, and relationships. We are promising you that you can eliminate all your negative emotions, all your addictions, all your relationship problems, and that you can live in positive emotions, in serenity and joy all the time. However, there is a price to pay.

The Price of Power

It is an ancient axiom that "Knowledge is Power". There is a price for power: learning, acquiring knowledge, achieving understanding of what things are and how they work. The power to transform your life is no exception.

With this book, you will be studying a new science, Psycanics. **Psycanics is the physics and electronics of trans-physical energy and realities**. Your trans-physical energies are those that you perceive directly in your consciousness, not through your physical body. They are not physical energies, you cannot measure out a kilo or a meter of emotions, or catch your thoughts in a bucket. Your trans-physical energies include:

> All your emotions, positive and negative.

> All thoughts and mental activities: programs, paradigms, beliefs, determinations, values, goals, imaginations, memories, etc.

> All your identities, your beliefs about who and what you are.

> All your motivations and impulses to behaviors, including addictions, compulsions, obsessions, and phobias.

> All your relationship energies: likes and aversions, love<>hate, acceptance<>rejection, inclusion<>exclusion, and how you treat others.

> Your happiness or unhappiness, non-physical pain and suffering.

This book is not inspirational. It is not motivational. It is not for entertainment purposes; it has no amusing stories. It is not a quick nor a light read. It is not an easy read. This book is hard science, a new science, a science of trans-physical energy and human non-physical experience. It is a science of how your interior life really works. It is a new psychology of the human being. This book is packed with new concepts and terminology to represent them. Many of those concepts and most of the terminology will be new to you. **Some of them will contradict what you now believe about life.** When it does, pay special attention because you are looking at your errors of thinking that are causing your problems in life.

There are three books in this series of Self Therapy. Mastering all three will give you more knowledge and understanding of human psychology and more power to produce easy and fast change than university degree in psychology.

Are you willing to pay the price for power, to learn a science?

Some of the Laws of Study and Learning:

Study is understanding. Just looking at information or reading it without fully understanding it, is not studying. The secret to understanding is to understand every word. It is not ideas that are mis-understood, but the words that express the idea.

Learning is acquiring the ability to act and produce the desired results. If you cannot produce results with what you studied, you have not learned no matter how much you studied. **It is very common that people study a lot and learn very little.**

You will be learning a new science of the non-physical energies that comprise your internal experience of thoughts, emotions, motivations, behaviors, and relationships. This science consists of terms, ideas, and concepts, some of which are as revolutionary to paradigms today as quantum mechanics was to Newtonian mechanics. For example: **you are the creator** of everything in your life; absolutely everything, both your internal, psycanic experience and your external, physical events and circumstances. Notice how that totally contradicts paradigms today that we live in an indifferent or even hostile world created by who knows what and over which we have very little control.

The concepts in psycanics are represented, symbolized, with technical terms and abbreviations, denoted with the abbreviation "TT" for "Technical Term". Usually these words are defined when first introduced. Any time you are in doubt about the meaning of a TT, you should look it up in the glossary. **You cannot use an ordinary dictionary to understand the TT's of psycanics:** that will produce confusion and sabotage your understanding.

We recommend reading the book twice because psycanics is a spherical science rather than linear. Many concepts are connected to other concepts and cannot be understood until all its connections are understood. Thus, there are concepts in the beginning which cannot be fully understood until later concepts are understood. Reading the book a second time will make much clearer the concepts in the first part of the book. Furthermore, this book contains too much information of sufficient complexity to be grasped with only one reading. On the first reading, you may go past things that you do not fully understand. However, on the second reading, **never go past any idea you do not fully understand.** If there is something you do not understand, look for mis-understood words. It is not ideas that are mis-understood; it is the words that comprise them. When you do not understand an idea, looks for one or more mis-understood ideas in the idea or the text previous to the idea.

Taxonomy

All science is taxonomic: there is a hierarchy of concepts from beginning and basic, to advanced and complex. Failing to understand a basic concept will impossibilitate (make impossible) learning the later, more advanced concepts. If, on your second reading of the book, everything is not clear, you have misunderstood words=concepts. **You are in the Domino Effect,** explained below.

The Snowball Effect

On studying any subject, that subject should become clearer and easier as you advance. This is the Snowball Effect: as you advance you "pick up" *with understanding* new concepts. They "stick" to and grow the Snowball of your understanding and eventual mastery of the subject.

The Domino Effect

The Domino Effect is the opposite of the Snowball Effect. **If any subject becomes more confusing and difficult as you try to advance in it, you are in the Domino Effect.** You are familiar with how pushing over the first domino in a line of dominoes causes each one to fall in succession.

The Domino Effect is the phenomenon that the first misunderstood word or concept in a subject will impossibilitate the understanding of later, more advanced concepts, which in turn will impossibilitate the comprehension of the even more advanced and complex concepts. Like a line of falling dominos, the first misunderstood word or idea produces more and more misunderstood ideas and makes them impossible to understand without clearing up all the previous misunderstoods. The result is the student snarls himself up in a mass of confusion and inability to master the subject. He usually abandons the study as a subject too advanced for his intellectual ability. We see this happen every day in the educational system: students give up on their education (whether or not they continue physically present in classes).

However, the problem is not the intelligence of the student. It is not that the subject is too advanced or difficult. The problem is that the student study technique is deficit. The true cause of the inability to master a subject is that the person proceeded to "study" beyond a misunderstood word or idea. **Just one misunderstood word is sufficient to initiate the Domino Effect.** We put "study" in quotes, because immediately that a person fails to understand, they are failing to study.

Illustration: The Domino Effect: The first mis-understood word or idea will impossibilitate the understanding of subsequent, more advanced ideas, which will impossibilitate the understanding of the subsequent, even more advanced ideas. The entire science becomes an area of confusion impossible to master.

You have probably experienced both effects yourself:

A- **What subjects have you studied that became easier and easier as you progressed?** In those subjects you are operating in the Snowball Effect.

B- **What subjects became more confusing and harder as you progressed?** In those subjects you were studying in the Domino Effect. You may even be able to remember the exact words or concepts that you never fully understood. When you continued ahead in your study with those poorly understood words or ideas, your Domino Effect began.

Some subjects, like science and math, are inherently more complex than others. But this does not change the principle that you master any subject by mastering each word and idea and operation in the taxonomy of that subject. The failure to master a word <u>at the moment</u> of encountering in the taxonomy starts up the Domino Effect.

When you find yourself reading with a blank mind, mechanically, without mental images and clear comprehension, you are in the Domino Effect. You must go back to where you were duplicating the information well and work forward to where your mind blankness began by carefully clearing the meanings of all words.

The price of psycanic magic, over power over your life, is first complete understanding and then practice in applying the knowledge until you can discreate your negative identities (NEIRs). We will hold you hand while you do this. But it all starts with your intellectual understanding of what to do, why to do it, and how to do it, which is the purpose of this book.

Law of Learning

If you cannot apply information and produce the desired results, you have not learned -- no matter how much you have studied.

Results = Learned.   Poor results = not learned.

To assist your understanding, we will often spell the technical terms (TT) of psycanics with a capital first letter. Examples: Cause, Game, Drama, Victim, Responsability, Space, Love. (Responsability (TT) is spelled with an "a" instead of "i".) You must learn the Psycanics' definitions and concepts for its Technical Terms (abbreviation: TT). If you apply the definition from an ordinary dictionary, you are guaranteed to have misunderstood words and will fall into the Domino Effect.

To support you in achieving the true learning of the BTT energy processing system in this book, you have:

#1- The Psycanics Being Transformation Technology (BTT) Course (online). This course provides step-by-step exercises to practice the many skills you need to do your self-therapy.

#2- Online support groups where professional pilots will guide you in applying the technology and discreating exactly what you need to discreate to change your life. You will learn, not only by your work on yourself, but also by observing the BTT processes of others.

4- Transformation

You can use the science of psycanics and its Being Transformation Technology as presented in this book to change **any specific** negative situation in your life: emotions, self-image, self-esteem, behaviors, addictions, traumas, fears, phobias, PTSD, blocks to taking action, relationship problems, etc. Once you learn Being Transformation Technology, changing any specific thing -- for example, eliminating a trigger and its negative emotions, or eliminating an addiction -- only takes an hour or two.

However, just discreating one negative emotion is like using battleship cannons to sink rowboats. **Psycanics and its Being Transformation Technology have the power to transform every aspect of your life**. The following table presents characteristics of what we mean by **Life Transformation**:

Table of Life Transformation

The Experience of the ordinary human being UHB = Unenlightened Human Being. ⬇	The Experience of a Transformed BEing. SEB = Spiritually Enlightened Being ⬇
Believes that he lives in a universe of dead matter over which he has little control.	Knows he is the creator of his internal, psycanic experience; and manifestor of what he wants externally, in the FU.
Does not understand how his BEing: will, consciousness, mind, emotions, behaviors, love, happiness, and relationships really work. Has little control over any of them.	Knows that everything in his BEing operates according to exact laws and principles. Applies the laws to control all elements of his BEing. Discreates all negative energies in his BEing and creates the positives he wishes to experience.
Believes his life is determined by randomity, coincidences, accidents, and bad luck.	Knows life is Cause→Effect. Lives consciously creating his desired results, in control of his life and satisfaction.
Lives in Game Conditions → poor results → **Drama**. Lots of Drama in his life.	Lives manifesting his desired results easily and in all Arenas of his life, ergo lives **FREE of all Drama**.
Frequently feels himself the victim of other people, events, or life itself. Lives blaming such externals for his problems and pains.	Lives at Cause and in 100% Responsability for his life and everything that happens within it. Never feels himself victim of anybody or anything.

Believes that his emotions (MODs and UPS) are caused by external events. Waste his energy trying to control externals to control his emotions.	Knows he is the absolute creator of his emotions and has permanently discreated the negative ones.
His life is full of MODs and UPS. Experiences frequent activations of his negative emotions: anger, anxiety, fears, resentments, guilt, hate, sadness, depression, etc.	Has no negative emotions; he has discreated them. Lives in True Happiness; in serenity, peace, and joy all the time.
His life is full of the Don Quixote Behaviors. He burns great amounts of TE struggling to stop others and events from triggering his MODs and UPS. (This produces most of the problems in relationships.)	Nothing ever triggers his MODs: he has no NEIR masses to trigger. He lets others and life be as they are, and as they are not.
Has multiple compulsive behaviors and substance addictions (alcohol, tobacco, drugs, etc.)	Has discreated the NEIR masses that powered his compulsions and addictions. Now has none.
Has fears and blocks to taking action: writer's block, speaking in public, laziness, indiscipline, irresponsibility, changing jobs, starting a business, leaving a relationship, etc.	Discreates any blocks to action.
His life is dominated by the **External Quest** for Happiness: striving for and accumulating external things (MOPs), mirages of happiness. These always soon pass.	Has achieved True Happiness. He lives **Free** of the world. Needs nothing external for happiness; externals events neither cause him pain nor does he mistake them for happiness.
Often seeks acceptance, validation, approval, love from others. Sometimes sells out her destiny to please others.	Lives free of caring about what others think. Pursues her passions.

RELATIONSHIPS	RELATIONSHIPS
His relationships tend to be full of negative energy, problems, conflicts, and negative emotions. Each person frequently triggers the other.	His relationships are free of all negative energy and conflicts. They operate in serenity, harmony, love, and joy.
Each person tries to use, to change, the other person to control his psycanic experience, his BE-FEEL, to avoid MODs and feel loved.	Each person creates his BE-FEEL. Has no need for the other person to BE or DO anything to please or to avoid displeasing, ergo Liberty.
Has many programs (beliefs, expectations, demands) about how other people should BE and DO, in erroneous and impossible intents to control his own BEing and emotions.	Has no NEIR masses, ergo no triggers, ergo has **no programs** about how others should BE or DO. Controls his BEing and emotions directly.
Not only tries to control and change others, to get them to obey him, but **does so with negative energy, with anti-love.** (Don Quixote Behaviors).	Gives all others the Liberty to BE and DO as they please. Law: There is no Love that does not start with Liberty.
Others resist his control and negative energies, generating problems and conflicts in his relationships.	All relationships operate in harmony, love, win-win negotiation, and mutual support.
Jealousies and "ownership" of the other, trying to dictate, control, and restrict the other person.	In psycanic relationships, all jealousy is eliminated with BTT. No one tries to possess or control the other.
Communications frequently hold negative energy: anger, recriminations, invalidations, blaming. The result is conflicts and arguments.	Communications are always free of all negative emotions and of all other negative energies using BTT when needed. Negotiations are easy and quick.
No responsibility for the relationship. Each believes the other person is the cause of all	Each person operates in 100% of Responsability for the quality of the relationship = **200% of**

the problems; that the other person must change, not me.	**Responsability** present. To resolve problems, one changes hirself, not the other.
The relationship accumulates negative energy (anger, resentment, blame, resistances, recriminations, you-owe-me, etc.) **until it finally breaks.**	Each person uses BTT as needed to maintain his BEing free of all negative energy. The parties negotiate problems in serenity and love.
Most spouse relationships fail: There is a **90% failure rate.** About 50% end in divorce. In another 40%, the people stay together but in dissatisfaction and UPS.	Transformed Beings know how to end relationships in harmony and love.
The end of relationships is often with negative energy. Divorce is usually acrimonious.	Relationships are fluid, and when they end, they do so in appreciation and gratitude to the other person.

It takes about 400 hours of BTT to achieve all the above. Students in the Psycanics Science Institute usually achieve those results in about two years working on themselves about one hour per day.

You choose the level of work on your Self and your life you want: from just changing one particular emotion or behavior; to changing many things in your life; to complete Transformation of your life; to full spiritual Awakening and Realization of Essence. There is no good<>bad; should be<>should not be. Only options and choices. It is all up to you.

There are three kinds of people in life:

1- Those who make things happen;

2- Those who watch things happen; and

3- Those who ask, "What the hell happened?"

If it's to be; it's up to me.

Spiritual Transformation

There are two levels of Transformation: human and spiritual. Spiritual Transformation is an AWAKENING to **Who You Really Are, a spirit, an individualization of the One Essence**. You-psycan are asleep in your Human Dream. You are inside the Matrix of the Creation lost in your illusion of being only a human being – exactly as you planned and created before coming to Earth.

You AWAKEN when you have had enough glimpses of Who You Are so that:

#1- you are certain of the existence of your Self as an immortal spirit and of your origin: the One Essence and Creator of All That Is.

AND

#2- you begin and maintain spiritual work on your Self to transcend your illusion of human being and recover permanently your experience of Self as immortal spirit, and restore your perception and communication with Essence.

Awakening leads to the **spiritual experience that is the core of all religions**. In the west / Christianity it has been called the Kingdom of Heaven, the Garden of Paradise, Salvation, Redemption. In the west / Buddhism, Hinduism, Taoism, Zen, it is called Enlightenment, Realization, Satori, Nirvana, Samadhi, among others. It has also been called Cosmic Consciousness. Essentiality calls it Enlightenment.

When you are Enlightened, you have transcended the illusion that you are only a human being to live permanently in the experience of being an immortal spirit just visiting Earth. And you have recovered your perception, connection, and communication with Essence, i.e. the Creator, aka God. She is everywhere around you all the time; She is all things; She forms everything that exists out of Her own Love-Life-Energy. To live the Human Adventure, you had to block your innate, psycanic ability to perceive Her. But the Truth always is: She is the only thing that Truly exists, and you are part of Her; we all are; we are all ONE. (You transcend the illusion of human by discreating the Shell, explained elsewhere.)

Awakening is an intermediary state: you must either progress forward to Enlightenment or you will fall back to Sleep. Without commitment and action to expand and make permanent your Awakening, to achieve your Enlightenment; you will lose your Self again in your human identity.

Most psycans on the planet now (2020 AD) are still enchanted with their Human Experience, with exploring Drama and UPS, and so are not interested in Awakening and Enlightenment. And that is Perfect. You are immortal; you have all eternity to explore the infinity of the Creation. The Human Experience is just one theater, one Matrix, in that infinity. You-psycan are free to stay here and cycle through as many human incarnations as you please; you already have hundreds.

But eventually, you-psycan will tire of being far from Love and exploring the Negative Side of the Creation Polarity, of Drama and UPS. You will enter the Dark Night of the Old Soul, and will long for Home, to Return to the Infinite Love-Joy from which you come.

Enlightened, you are the end of your cycle of incarnations on Earth, of samsara (Hinduism). You return to the Creation integrated with Essence and can choose another Movie Matrix in the infinity of options of experience that is the Creation. Most options are unlike Earth in that they are positive-energy experiences and you do not lose your consciousness of Who You Are

All religions were intended to be Paths Back Home, back to Essence; but they have lost not only the understanding of the Goal as well as any effective and rapid technology to achieve it. Essentiality is a new statement of the universal Wisdom of the True Nature of Existence. It is a science of Essence and a system of Return to the One. Essentiality is a modern, western, scientific, precise, and relatively quick Path back to your True Self and your Essence. Where in other schools, enlightenment takes lifetimes, in Essentiality you can achieve it in five years.

Psycanics is a derivative of Essentiality; of Ultimate Spiritual Knowledge applied to your human life on Earth. While you need not know Who You Really Are (psycan-aware-will-creator), nor of the existence of Essence, it is most helpful to understand all that when you work on your Self psycanically. You will have much more power to create and discreate doing so from psycan rather than from your human identity.

Here is a table comparing some of the characteristics of Enlightenment, of SEBs (Spiritual Enlightened Beings) with UHBs: Unenlightened Human Beings.

An UHB is one who does not know:

1- Who He Really Is, which has two parts: #1- immortal spirit-ual BEing playing in the Creation; #2 an individualization and always part of the One Infinite Creator BEing who is also the Essence of the Creation

2- Does not know he is the creator of everything in his life and so lives in a paradigm of powerlessness, helplessness, and victim of external forces over which he believes he has little influence.

3- Is not aware that his subconscious primary creation for his life is struggle, Drama, and UPS (all the negative emotions).

Table of Spiritual Transformation

The Experience of the UHB: Unenlightened Human Being. ⬇	The Experience of an SEB: Spiritually Enlightened Being: ⬇
Lives with no perception/experience of the Creator, either blindly believing in a religion, or as an agnostic or atheist.	Can feel Essence and communicate with Her at will. Knows by personal experience exactly what God is, where She is, and is connected to Her.
The universe is a giant machine, if not hostile, at least indifferent to his plight.	The Creation is alive and is Infinite Love. The SEB trusts Love to always produce what is ultimately Perfect for him.
His spirituality is limited to the dead dogmas of churches and religions. Has no real knowledge or experience of Essence.	Knows that all is One Infinite Spirit. Experiences himself as an immortal spirit, part of the One Great Spirit who is Oneness, Power, Love-Joy.
Believes and experiences himself as only a human being, as a physical body with only lifetime.	Knows and experiences Self as an immortal spirit just visiting Earth to enjoy the Human Adventure Experience.
Lives in fear of death of self, and of loved ones.	Has processed his past lives. Knows he has "died" many times before; has no fear of death, nor is distressed when others "die".
Lives in separated, isolated individuality from others, and with the world divided into conflicting groups: "Us versus Them". Sadness and loneliness.	Perceives the ONE pervading all that exists. Feels Unity with all others and Life. Is never alone; Essence, Love, is always present in his experience. He is always HOME.

He drags a highly-charged past with him through life. That past contains painful memories, failures, traumatic incidents (violence, abuse, abandonment, etc.) embarrassments, relationships resentments, etc. The past is painful.	The transformed BEing has cleaned all negative energy from his past. He can recall or think on anything in his past with zero pain, but never does so without some good reason. He lives **Free of the Past.**
Believes the past shapes and limits him and he has limited capacity to change.	Knows the past has no power over his present. He has re-created himself in his ideal of BEing.
Is driven by negative ego: judges everyone as either better or worse, more or less, than he. Uses masks, pretensions, bragging, one-upmanship, ostentation, trying to convince others of superiority. Struggles to climb in hierarchies (the heights are always empty).	Knows we are all illusory individualizations of the One and that the negative ego is a hallucination: There is no more or less in One. Knows everyone is an equal child of the One. Lives Free of all egoic competition with others. Lives in Humility without which there is no Wisdom, Power, Love, or Happiness.
Continues to live in the original purpose of the Human Experience: Games Conditions → poor results → Drama.	Has chosen the High Road of Power→Results→Satisfaction Has great power to create and manifest in his FU what he wishes to experience.
In conclusion: **Life occurs in the Valley of Darkness and Tears, full of Drama and UPS.**	**In conclusion:** **Life is a Return to the Garden of Eden; to creation, ease, abundance, and constant enjoyment.**

5- Experience

Everything we have said until now is preliminaries. We now begin the study of psycanics itself. The only thing you do in life is to try to control your experience. However, how it really works is quite distinct to how humans think it works: Knowledge is Power.

"EXPERIENCE" (TT) is the most fundamental concept in all the Creation. Your experience is the only thing you have; the only thing you know. The Creation* is an infinity of experiences; your life is a parade of experiences. Understanding what experience is and how yours works are the keys to power over yourself, over life, and to being happy all the time. You are the creator of all your experience and can discreate your undesired ones (such as anger, depression, guilt, sorrow, addictions, traumas, PTSD, relationship conflicts, etc.). *(Creation with a capital "C" means everything that exists: all dimensions, all realities, all universes. Creation with a small "c" means any reality, any thing, that exists within the Creation.) Essence manifests the Creation filling it with an infinity of creations, all formed of Her Life Energy.)*

You are an experience for Essence and everything you experience, She experiences through you. You are also a sub-creator, expanding the Creation from within by all that you create and do in your life. Your human life is your creation, although as a human being you will not-know this so that you can create Drama and explore negative energy of all kinds (for example, negative emotions).

Purpose of Existence

The purpose of the Creation is Experience, every kind of experience possible without limits and including all negative experiences, Drama, and UPS. The Creation is Essence manifesting Her Self, Her Life Energy Essence, in all Her infinite possibilities and varieties of being; i.e. the Creation. The Creation is the playground, the Disneyland of Essence. The Creation is Essence exploring, experiencing and knowing Her Self in all Her infinite possibilities of BEing. This includes that She manifests Her Self as and explores all the negative polarities including evil. In the chapter on Polarity, we will explain why negative experiences such as pain, suffering, loss, and evil must exist. However, once you have experience them, you need not keep having them in your life.

The purpose of this planet is to host the Human Adventure Experiences. You are starring in yours now. The Human Experience is the exploration of negative energies of all kinds: problems, conflicts, victim, errors, poor results, failures, Drama, and all the negative emotions which are the essence of **U**nhappiness, **P**ain, and **S**uffering, abbreviate henceforth as **UPS**.

Consciousness

Consciousness is the power to perceive, experience, feel, and thereby to know. Consciousness is one of the 13 Primordial Characteristics of Essence; it exists before and outside of the Creation; it is a priori to all things. Consciousness is mystical; it is beyond human comprehension. Consciousness does not come from the physical universe (where so many sciences are seeking its origin). It does not come from your body or your brain or your mind.

Experience is consciousness in operation; consciousness being impacted by energies and realities producing those experiences.

Consciousness = perception, feeling, experiencing, ergo knowing.

You-spirit-psycan are an individualization of Essence with the same Characteristics, including consciousness. You are a **trans-physical=spiritual** entity of Aware-Will. Consciousness is part of your fundamental spirit-ual nature. It is your power to experience; you experience your psycanic energies directly in consciousness; you experience the physical universe through the senses of your body.

Many people have been seeking the origin of consciousness using such hypotheses as that it evolves within and from the physical universe; that it is chemical in nature; or that it is a product of the brain, etc. All of these are wrong. Consciousness is a priori to the physical universe. It is one of the 13 Primordial Characteristics of Essence, of the Creator Being. Consciousness is an aspect of the Creator of matter. It then incarnates within matter to play in and experience its creations.

What is Experience?

Experience is the impact (effect) of **realities** (modulated masses of energy) on consciousness. Experience is the perception, feeling, and thereby knowing of realities.

Experience is consciousness at work.

Definition: **Reality, Realities (TT)**: A reality is any form of energy being what it is. A reality is energy modulated, taking on a form, energy being some thing. A reality is energy taking on a specific form and identity. Everything that exists is a reality. Examples of physical realities: electron, atom, molecule, rock, tree, dog, human body, house, planet, star, galaxy, the entire physical universe: all are realities. Examples of psycanic realities: every thought, memory, idea is a reality. Every emotion is a reality. Your identities are realities. Your relationships are realities.

Realities Cause Experience.
Experience is the Effect of Realities (on consciousness).

To change your experience, create and discreate your realities.
(Do not resist your experience! Resistance Causes Persistence.)

The technical definitions are important because you are learning to control your experience by creating and discreating your psycanic realities, particularly your realities about yourself: your identities.

Your Three Dimensions of Experience

Your primary objective in life, your Existential Imperative, is to control your experience. Everything you do is to control your own experience. You seek to reduce and eliminate negative experiences (such as your negative emotions, addictions, relationships conflicts) which are UPS; and to produce positive experiences which are happiness. You are innately capable of doing this; you have the Power to do so. However, as a human being, you do not understand how your experience works, and the ways you are trying to control it now do not, cannot, and will not work. Psycanics shows you what you are doing that does not work and what you need to do to control your experience. The objective is that you achieve True Happiness, which is a state of only positive emotions (satisfaction, peace, enthusiasm, love, joy, etc.) all the time no matter what.

Your experience is everything that you perceive and feel and know, whether physical or trans-physical (psycanic). You have three dimensions of experience. As all experience is the effect of energy, of realities, on consciousness, you have three dimensions of very different kinds of energy.

Your three major fields, dimensions, worlds, or universes of energy-experience are:

1- Spiritual   2- Psycanic   3- Physical

Illustration: Your three dimensions/universes of experience, shown vertically and horizontally.

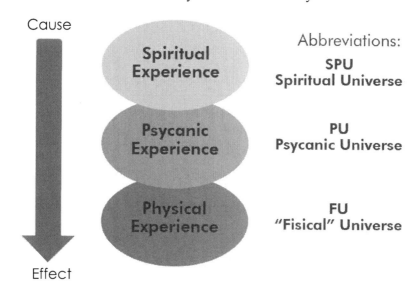

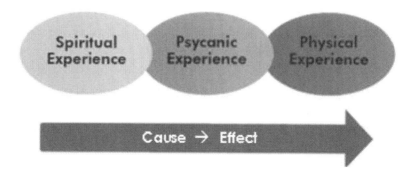

#1- Physical Universe (FU) Experience

Your **physical experience** is everything you perceive of the physical universe, of physical energies and matter. You have a physical body and experience it. Through the instrument of your body and its five senses, you perceive, you experience, the external, physical world.

- Negative physical experience is physical pain or suffering.
- Positive physical experience is physical pleasure.

Positive physical experiences are NOT happiness! Most people confuse g the enjoyment of physical experiences (e.g. travel, vacations) with happiness. Happiness is a positive *emotional* state all the time no matter what; physical pleasures always come and go. One of the great errors of the human being is chasing the mirage of happiness in the form of physical experiences. Pleasure and happiness are not at all the same thing, something we will examine in depth later.

———————————————————-

2- Your Psycanic Universe (PU) Experience

You are a **psycan**, a nonphysical, life-energy entity, a spirit. You are formed of Consciousness (Awareness) and Will (and the other 11 Characteristics of Essence, of which 4 are critical to your human existence). You are an immortal, spirit entity of **Aware-Will**. You-psycan are incarnating in a human identity complex and a human body to play in the Creation. You are currently visiting Earth and starring in your Human Drama Movie.

You are consciousness. Consciousness is the ability, the power, to perceive and experience realties. The Creation consists of an infinity of realities; everything that exists is a reality. All realities are creations: some one, some where, some time, had to create them for them to exist. For your life experiences, that someone is you. In this book and throughout psycanics, we will be explaining and proving HOW you create everything in your life

Definition: Your psycanic experience is all your nonphysical or trans-physical, energies that you-psycan experience directly in your consciousness, rather than through your body. They are non-physical, trans-physical energies: they cannot be captured or measured with physical instruments. **They do not come from and are not part of the physical universe.**

You have multiple kinds of psycanic energies-experiences including

- emotions,
- thoughts and memories and all mental activities and experiences,
- identities (your creations of self, what you are and are not),

- motivations, impulses, and compulsions to behaviors (such as addictions);

- your communication and relationship energies (such as like◇dislike), which either produce harmony and love, or problems and conflicts.

For example, like◇dislike, love◇hate, and Happiness◇UPS are psycanic energy-experience polarities. (Polarity has a chapter later.)

The word "experience" in psycanics will always refer _psycanic_ experience unless otherwise stated. When we use the word "experience" without qualifiers such as "past", "physical", "spiritual"; we always mean your **psycanic** experience: identities, emotions, thoughts, behaviors, relationship energies (such as affinity and aversions), love, drama, and happiness.

————————————————————-

Psycanic Experience A- Emotions

Of all your psycanic energies-creations, your identities are by far the most powerful. However, the energies of which you are probably most aware are your emotions, especially the negative ones which are not only the essence of UPS; they are the ONLY UPS that exist for you.[1]

Your emotions are your **self-love energies,** positive and negative, determined by your Essence Identity of the moment. (You will not understand this until much later in the book.)

Examples of positive emotions include: contentment, satisfaction, interest, respect, enthusiasm, affection, passion, and joy. They are happiness itself.

Examples of negative emotions include: anger, frustration, impatience, anxiety, fear, resentment, guilt, sadness, sorrow, loneliness, hate, apathy, depression, etc. Again, these are the only UPS (Unhappiness, Pain, and Suffering) that exist.

Until you understand that your emotions are the only Happiness or UPS that exist and learn what they are, how they work, how to discreate the negative ones, and how to create positive ones; you do not understand, nor will you be able to achieve True Happiness. All this is what we are teaching you in the three books of the Self Therapy series.

---

1 (Reminder: In psycanics, UPS (Unhappiness, Pain, and Suffering) and "negative experience" always refer to your psycanic experience, to mental and emotional pain, never to physical pain unless "physical" is specified.)

Law:

Your own negative emotions are the only UPS that exist for you.
Your UPS is never what happens (external events),
but what you <u>FEEL</u> (your emotions) in relation to events.

You will NEVER be able to always control what happens.
You can learn to always control your emotions – and that
is all that you need to achieve True Happiness.

Psycanic Experience B- Thoughts

All your mental realities such as thoughts, memories, ideas, concepts, knowledge, mental images and visualizations, beliefs, programs, paradigms, values, determinations, opinions, judgments. etc. All thoughts are mental energy forms, mental realities, your mental creations.

Your psycanic mental experience also includes your mental activities and operations such as remembering, cogitating, analyzing, counting, calculating, contemplating, theorizing, speculating, imagining, designing, and planning.

The totality of your mental realities and mental operations is the MIND.
There is no such thing as a mind as a separate entity; there is only you-psycan-aware-will creating, manipulating, and experiencing your mental creations-realities. However, we will continue to use "mind" as if there were such a thing to refer to your mental operations and realities.

Psycanic Experience C- Identities

Your identities are the most powerful realities in your life. They determine all the other aspects of your life (through the Causal Sequence). Your identities are your creations (which become your beliefs) about what you are and what you are not. They comprise your self-image and determine your self-esteem. They form your BEing, all that you are being and are not being.

This book is about learning to discreate your negative identities and re-creating yourself in positive ones, thereby to transform our will and will and your BEing. As your BEing is the only causal element in your life, recreating your BEing will transform your entire life. This works like magic, and we shall see that it is an exact science.

Psycanic Experience: D- Other

We consider your behaviors psycanic because, although your actions are physical, your impulses, motivations and reasoning for them are psycanic. You can change any behavior by changing the psycanic energy (an identity) driving it.

We consider your relationships psycanic because, although hugs and sex are physical, your thoughts, communications, feelings, and love are psycanic. You can change anything in your relationships, or transform them completely, by changing the psycanic energies (identities) that control them.

#3- Spiritual Experience

You are an immortal spiritual being -- technical term "psycan" -- enjoying a Human Adventure in which you-psycan are living the illusion of being a human. You-psycan are enjoying your Human Movie (just like you-human go to Hollywood movies for the drama). You are the writer, director, and star of your Human Adventure Movies. You have blocked your consciousness of your true spiritual BEing because that much Wisdom, Power, and Love, and Joy would ruin the Human Drama for you. Thus, few humans have any real spiritual experience, neither of themselves as spirits nor of the Creator, Essence of all that is.

No true spiritual experience is not an accident: it is a creation, your creation. You cannot truly live the Human Experience if you know Who You Really Are. In psycanics and Essentiality, we detail how you create your "avidya", the Hinduism and Buddhism term for spiritual ignorance of Who You Really Are and how life really works. One of the main differences between UHBs (Unenlightened Human Beings) and SEBs (Spiritual Enlightened Beings) is avidya versus the experience and knowing of Who You Really Are.

When humans do not have an actual connection and communication with Essence, they create mental structures, belief systems, i.e. religions. Religions are a poor substitute for personal experience of Essence, who is Infinite Love-Joy. It is **always within your power to recover your spiritual experience** including perception and communication with the One Essence of all that is (i.e. God). Essentiality is a system for recovering your experience of yourself as a "child of Essence" able to perceive and communicate with Essence. Again, graduates of the Essentiality School of Accelerated Enlightenment have achieved this level of consciousness.

Here are the six of the Laws of Experience, followed by discussion:

1- **All your experience is your creation.** There is nothing in your emotions, mind, identities, or behaviors that you did not create. Your Human Illusion requires you to believe the opposite: that you are **not** the creator of your experience but that external events are. Your ignorance and blindness to your True Creator Power is also your creation.

2- **What you have created, you can discreate,** i.e. cause to not-exist, so you can create positive experience in its place. Your Human Illusion requires you to resist your negative realities so they persist thereby producing lots of Drama (TT) in your life.

3- **You cannot create positive over the top of negative already present in your BEing.** You must first discreate the negatives, upon which the positive will shine forth unopposed, easily, and permanently. In other word, it does not work to try to plaster positive creations over negatives; the negatives will always poke through. Therefore, any therapy that focuses on trying to create positives without first discreating the negatives will have very limited results. *(We know of no other system of therapy that efficiently discreates negatives.)* Discreating negatives is not all that hard; you are learning how with this book.

4- **Your emotions are the only happiness or UPS that you know.** Your happiness or UPS is NEVER what happens but how you FEEL, your emotions, positive or negative, about what happens (events). As we will prove, external events are **never** the cause of your emotions.

5- Your happiness (emotions) does not depend on anything in your external world. **Nothing in the external world ever causes your emotions. NEVER, EVER.** As long as you keep believing — hallucinating — that external events determine your emotions and therefore cause your UPS or can produce your happiness, you will not be able to control your emotions or ever be much happier than you are now.

6- **The only thing that you have to do to be happy all the time no matter what happens in your life, is discreate your masses of negative identities-emotions (NEIR masses)** that reside latent in your subconsciousness and keep triggering over and over into your consciousness-experience producing your UPS. Once the negative identities are discreated, it is then easy to create and maintain positive identities-emotions which will produce the positive emotions that are happiness. Again, we are going to show you how to do all this in this book.

Discreation of Realities

Laws:

The Creation consists of realities.
Realities cause experience.
Experience is the effect of realities (on consciousness).

To change your experience, discreate the causal reality and create your desired one. Instead of discreating the negative reality, UHBs resist their negative experience. Thus, they live resisting effects instead of addressing and changing the causes. **Resistance to your negative experience will cause persistence of that experience.** All this we will see in great detail later, especially in Book 2. Understanding all this is crucial to your power over your life and your happiness.

Life

Your life is your experience. You know ONLY your experience. You have nothing but your experience. (Notice how the dead have no experience, at least of this world.)

Your life is a parade of experiences of five kinds, Six Arenas: BE→FEEL→THINK→RELATE /DO→HAVE (explained in the next chapter). The only way you can have no experience is to not exist — and this is impossible. When you die, your human experience ceases to exist but you-psycan, the Aware-Will entity that you are, continue. You-psycan are as immortal as Essence: you are Essence. However, you will reincarnate here on Earth until your discreate the Shell that holds you here in the Human Adventure Theater.

The Existential Imperative

The Existential Imperative of human existence is:

The ultimate motivation of all human behavior is to control
one's own experience; to avoid or stop negative experience (UPS)
and to produce positive experience (pleasure and happiness.)

The ONLY thing you do in life is try to control your experience.
You try to avoid or stop unpleasant experiences, and to produce pleasant ones.

The underlying motivation of all human behavior is one's own happiness.

Every human being is 100% selfish all the time, and cannot be otherwise. (We can prove this.) This is only a problem when a person does not understand the true nature of existence and happiness. Of course, this ignorance is the state of all UHBs. The result is all the negative conditions, problems and conflicts, and suffering we have on the planet. Again, none of this is accident: the exploration of negative conditions, evil, and UPS is the purpose of this reality matrix.

We all seek to avoid or stop negative experience, UPS (unhappiness, pain, and suffering), and to produce positive experience, pleasure, and happiness. People will say that they are motivated by many things, including love for others, but in the ultimate, scientific analysis, they are always motivated, consciously or subconsciously, by how they think their decisions will make them feel.

The ways a normal human being tries to control his experience DO NOT WORK. Not only do they not work, they persist and intensify negative experience and create Drama (TT) and UPS, for self and for others.

Games

Definition: **Game: A Game is all effort and struggle to overcome obstacles to** reach a goal.

Life is a Game. Every activity in your life is a Game. The Creation is a Game Field, a playing field for Games. Games are a very rich kind of Experience, and Experience, you remember, is the Purpose of the Creation. The Creation is Essence being the Creation and playing with and in it. You are one of the players.

The essence of a Game is NOT the achievement of the goals! It is not about winning. The essence of a Game is all the **experience** of struggling with the obstacles to overcome them. Remember: Experience is the purpose of all existence, of the Creation. The vast majority of the experience (the purpose of a Game) is in the struggle, not in getting the goal.

Every time you want something, every time you set a goal, every time you have an ongoing activity with a purpose; you are engaged in a Game. Common human Games include: getting educated; work, jobs, and career; success; relationships; getting married; having and then raising children; money and wealth creation; accumulating possessions and properties, staying healthy, social status; and power, fame and fortune. You-psycan are an immortal spirit temporarily incarnating on Earth to play Games, a very rich form of experience which -- please always remember -- is the purpose of the Creation and you incarnating within it.

The essence of a Game is not the goal. The essence of a Game is the struggle to overcome the obstacles (to the goal). Note how sports are the players' efforts to overcome obstacles (often the opposing players) and score the goal. Note how good movies are about hero's struggles to overcome great problems and challenges and achieve their desired results. The essence of your life experience is not your goals, but everything you must do to achieve them. Your richest and long-lasting life experiences are much more the DO-ing (effort to achieve goals) than the HAVE-ing of the goals.

The concept of Game includes movies. Movies are the stories of Games. In good movies, the hero always faces and struggles to overcome obstacles to some goal. **Your life is your Human Movie** and consists of all your Games, all your goals in life.

Your Life and Everything in it is a Game.

You-psycan are here on Earth to play Games.

Game Conditions

The greatest amount and richest experience in a Game is during the effort to overcome the obstacle. The experience of getting the goal, celebration of a goal, is of secondary importance and is very short compared with the struggle against the obstacle.

Game Conditions exist when you have the circumstances necessary **to keep a Game going by not winning it, by not producing the desired results (goals).** If you achieve your goals, it is GAME OVER. Now what are you going to do for fun?

Game conditions exist when you have a goal, an obstacle to it, and a balance of power between the player and the obstacle so that the **personal power of the player is insufficient** to overcome the obstacles and achieve the goal. **By not-winning your Games, you-psycan keep your** Games=*experiences of challenge= experience of aliveness* – albeit mostly negative-- going. Remember, experience is your purpose: Your Games (effort and struggle) are your main experience; winning and losing are secondary experiences.

As you-psycan in Essence are an immortal spirit-ual entity with the full Creator Power of Essence, you must counter-create Who You Really Are to be a human being and live in Game Conditions. Again, in psycanics and Essentiality, we detail how you do this so that you can reverse the process and transform to manifesting your desired results in life instead of Game Conditions.

To more fully understand Game and Game Conditions, you need to understand Drama (TT). (We will capital "D" Drama to remind you that it is a TT with a very specific definition in psycanics.)

Law of Experience

The primary experiential purpose of Games and Game Conditions is Drama (TT). You-psycan came to Earth for the Drama.

Drama

**The purpose of Games is Experience.
One of the richest forms of Experience is Drama.**

Do you have lots of drama in your life? Is your life dramatic?

Drama is a major concept in psycanics and the Human Experience. You-psycan as a UHB are (unconsciously) creating Drama in your life, which means you are creating **not-HAVE-ing** your desired results in many areas of your life. You are sabotaging your innate Power of Manifestation to create and maintain Game Conditions which produce Drama instead of results.

DRAMA (TT) is all the varied and rich experience, *mostly negative,* that we savor during a Game (and therefore in movies).

Drama includes: effort, struggle, problems, conflicts, uncertainty, doubt, suspense, frustration, impotence, impatience, anxiety, fear, anger, rage, desperation, depression, allies and enemies, loyalty and betrayal, losing and winning, victory and defeat, failure, sadness and sorrow, elation and despair, regret, guilt, giving up or perseverance, etc.: a great variety of tasty experiences.

The purpose of the Creation is Experience. Drama is a very rich kind of experience – albeit mostly negative. By the Laws of Polarity, you must alternate your polarity of experience to refresh and renew your capability to savor and appreciate your experience. Notice that if your experience were positive all the time, you would eventually become bored with it. The truth is, that as a spiritual being, you seek to alternate your experience. You seek both positive and negative; either all the time, would eventually be boring, even unbearable. You seek challenge and excitement, i.e. Game Conditions and Drama.

Drama is mostly UPS

Notice that Drama includes all the negative emotions, and **therefore is mostly UPS (unhappiness, pain, and suffering),** interspersed with brief celebrations on achieving some goal. We will use the abbreviation **DUPS** to represent **Drama, Unhappiness, Pain, and Suffering** as being intimately related.

**The Purpose of Games (and movies) is Drama.
The Purpose of the Human Adventure is
to explore and savor Drama.**

Is your life Dramatic? Congratulations! You are a powerful and successful creator of Drama. You-psycan incarnated into the Human Game for the Drama. You create and keep yourself in *Game Conditions→Drama* by suppressing your innate, divine Creator Power so that you do not easily and quickly manifest your desired results / goals in life. Thus, you keep the Game going and the Drama coming.

Unenlightened Human Beings (UHBs) are *subconsciously* creating Drama instead of results. Spiritual Enlightened Beings (SEBs) know Who They Really Are, understand life and how creation works, and *consciously* create results, serenity, love and joy instead of Drama.

How You Create and Maintain Drama

You create and maintain Drama in your life by maintaining Game Conditions which are all efforts to overcome obstacles. To maintain Game Conditions and therefore keep the Drama going, you must not achieve your goals. As long as you do not reach a goal, the Game continues and so the Drama continues.

Reach a goal and it is **Game Over** which is **End of Drama**. Bummer; now what are you-psycan going to do for experience? You would have to find another Game. Best to keep the old ones going as long as possible and suck all the Drama possible out of them. Thus, we struggle with the same goals (Games) for years and years = live long-term Dramas. Examples of common human Dramas include health, success, money, relationships, and happiness.

Unenlightened Human Beings (UHBs) are subconsciously playing Games while sabotaging their Results so that the Game continues and they can savor the Drama. Of course, if you confront most people with this fact, they will deny that they are creating Drama instead of Results – which denial is itself great Drama.

One of the fundamental ways you-psycan create and maintain Drama is by denying and not-knowing you are the creator. Denying creator kills your personal power. (Definition: Power (TT) The ability to produce your desired results.) If you were being Powerful Creator, you would manifest your goals quickly and it would be Game Over. In Book 2, we will have chapters on Creator and Responsability. Until you acknowledge and take Responsability that you are the creator of your Dramas, you will have no Power to exit them into Results. Denial of being the creator of your Dramas maintains you in Drama.

No Results→ Drama is NOT Bad-SNB!

Definition: Bad-SNB: acronym for <u>**Bad = that which Should Not Be.**</u> Bad is anything that you have decided Should Not Be, Should Not Exist or Should Not Exist as it is. Your opinion of Bad-SNB *apparently* justifies your use of negative energy to attack and stop, change, punish of destroy that Bad-SNB reality. Your psycanic neg-energy (such as anger) are your only UPS in life. All your UPS in life comes from your creations (opinions) of Bad-SNB.

Bad-SNB is a hallucination: there is nothing Bad-SNB in the entire Creation. Thus, you generate your UPS and suffer because you hallucinate. We will explain this fully in Book 2.

DUPS (Drama, Unhappiness, Pain, and Suffering) are **NOT** **Bad-SNB!** They are valid and rich experiences. The Creation would be the poorer without them. You-psycan came to Earth, to the Human Experience, to explore and enjoy DUPS. There is nothing that is Bad-SNB; everything is a valid experience. The purpose of the Creation is ALL experiences possible, without exception. There are two reason why nothing is Bad-SNB:

1. As the negative polarity side of happiness, DUPS must exist. Furthermore, you-psycan must explore DUPS at some time in your existence to appreciate happiness (this is a Law of Polarity). However, as a human being now, you had many lifetimes in DUPS and you need not continue living in DUPS when you have had enough of it and know how to get out (which is what we are teaching you in this book).

2. Second, all negative experience (DUPS) is rich and valid. The Creation is divinely designed to include absolutely all possibilities and varieties of experience including all polarities and all negatives, including evil. The Creation would be impoverished were there are no negative experience. In fact, it could not function at all as we will see when we get to the Laws of Polarity.

You-psycan incarnated on Earth to explore Drama and UPS, which are the negative polarity of Wisdom, Power, Love and Joy, your divine nature. To come to Earth and be human and enjoy DUPS, you-psycan had to counter create your spiritual nature of Essence, of Wisdom, Power, Value, Love- Joy (WPVLJ). You had to encase yourself in psycanic realities, in psycanic mass, to reduce your consciousness down to that of a human being (very low on the Cosmic scales of BEing).

You cannot explore Drama in your true psycanic (spiritual) nature: You are too wise and too powerful. In your true psycanic nature you are Essence; you are Wisdom, Power, Value, and Love-Joy, abbreviated WPVLJ and pronounced "Whipple".

You counter-created your WPVLJ with NEIRs: Negative Essence Identity Realities. These identities are the root of all your DUPS in life. This book is about:

1- how to find your Essence counter-creations in your subconscious.

2- how to discreate them using the Psycanics' Being Transformation Technology (BTT).

3- how to re-create yourself in positive identities that affirm your spiritual nature of WPVLJ: Wisdom, Power, Value, Love-Joy.

Changing your BEing so will transform your entire life into Wisdom, Power, Results, Love, and Joy.

Control of your Experience

The Existential Imperative declares that the underlying motivation of all your efforts and behaviors in life is to control your experience. However:

**You will never be able to always
control your external events and circumstances.**

You cannot control what others do and say, nor many of the events of life (accidents, sickness, losing your job, divorce, etc.). The nature of life for everyone, no matter how powerful or rich a person may be, is that you win some and you lose some.

However:

**You can always control your internal, psycanic experience: your
emotions, thoughts, and above all your identities
(which determine your self-image and self-esteem.)
These are all your creations.**

**Controlling your psycanic experience is the
only thing you need to do to be Truly Happy (TT).
(Remember: True Happiness is positive emotional state
all the time no matter what.)**

**Controlling your psycanic experience is the only thing
you CAN do to be Truly Happy – and it is the only thing necessary.**

Your Emotions

Your own negative emotions (abbreviated neg-emo) **are the only UPS** that exist for you. Your happiness or UPS in life is *never* what is, or occurs, in your life, but rather **how you FEEL** in relation to the events. (We will see later it is actually how you BE in relation to events, and how your BE determines your FEEL.)

A simple example: A person's father dies (an event). Some people will grieve when their father dies; others will be glad (they hated their father, or they get an inheritance); others are indifferent. Same event, three different experiences. Your happiness or UPS is your FEEL-ings, not the event.

Your only UPS in life is your own negative emotions.
Your negative emotions are your only UPS in life.

Your UPS is never the events, but how
you FEEL about the events.

Cause of Your Psycanic Experience

External things and events cause your experience of the physical world. In the same way, your internal, psycanic realities cause your psycanic experience. You-psycan are living in a Shell of energy that contains millions of psycanic realities which act upon you-consciousness to generate your psycanic experience, including your experience of being only a human being.

You-psycan live in a psycanic universe just as you-human live in a physical universe. Both universes consist of realities causing experience. However, there is no causal relationship between the physical universe (FU) and your psycanic universe (PU).

External events are NEVER the cause of your psycanic experience, of your FEELings=your emotions. External events are NEVER the cause of your UPS, nor can they ever produce your happiness. No amount of money or external things can ever produce True Happiness, good relationships, or love-joy. No amount of external riches can ever compensate your internal, negative psycanic realities that cause all your UPS in life.

External Events are NEVER the cause of
your internal, psycanic experience.

There are no wires, cables, remote control, wi-fi, Bluetooth, telepathy, witchcraft, or voodoo between the physical universe and your internal psycanic world. In the same way that nobody can cause you to think or believe anything, to change religions or politics; nothing external causes or can cause your feelings and emotions.

Nothing external in your life ever causes your psycanic experience.

Lower energies (physical energy and matter) never control higher energies (your psycanic ones). Higher ones control lower ones: for example: your will is your highest energy and can control your lower energies of thoughts and emotions (you are learning how in this book). Your will can even manifest things and events in your physical life.

If events caused psycanic experience; everyone would have the same experience for the same event. The opposite is true: for any given event, human experience will vary greatly, from very negative to very positive. This is the law of Consistency of Cause which we will see later.

If events were the cause of psycanic experience, there would be no hope for True Happiness. Nobody can always control events, and Life is a polarity: there are always positive and always negative events for every person.

Life is a parade of events. Always some are positive and some negative from any given POV (Point of View). The parade of your life will unfold as it does, you have only limited input. **Your job is to be HAPPY all the time no matter what Life does.** Life is NOT the problem for your happiness; you are. Your problem with happiness is not what Life does, but understanding how your psycanic experience works and taking control of it.

True Cause of UPS

In this book we will show you exactly what does cause your negative emotions, your UPS, and how to discreate them to achieve True Happiness. The True Cause of your negative emotions are your Negative Essence Identity Realities, your NEIRs. *(To be explained in their own chapter.)*

This is great news because **to be happy all the time no matter what, you only need to control your psycanic experience, your identities and emotions.** You need not control the external world and its events — which are impossible to control anyway. And when you do learn to control your psycanic experience, you will find you have much, much more control over your external world, including your relationships and your power to manifest what you want in your physical dimension.

You cannot control your external world (FU) until you learn to control your internal world (PU). Your PU determines your FU as shown by the Causal Sequence.

End of Chapter

Review of Technical Terms of Psycanics

True Happiness: a state of positive emotions (satisfaction, enthusiasm, passion, joy, love, etc.) pretty much all the time, unaffected by external events, fame or fortune. True Happiness is a state of BEing and FEELing (BE-FEEL) impregnable to external events and conditions.

UPS: abbreviation for <u>U</u>nhappiness, <u>P</u>ain, and <u>S</u>uffering, pronounced "oops". UPS includes all the negative emotions: anger, frustration, impotence, anxiety, fear, guilt, sorrow, regret, resentment, loneliness, hate, and depression, to name a few. UPS is the polarity opposite of Happiness. Synonyms: neg-emotion, neg-emo.

UPS in psycanics always refer to negative psycanic experience, to mental and emotional pain, unless physical pain or suffering is specified.

Activation: the triggering and jump of a NEIR mass from the subconscious to consciousness-experience. It is felt primarily as neg-emo, but the NEIR is always there inside the neg-emo. Synonym: MOD: Moment of Dolor (Pain).

MOD: Moment of Dolor. (Dolor is Latin for pain.) Synonym for activation: the movement of a mass of neg-emo from your subconscious to your consciousness=experience.

External events (or just "events"): A very general word meaning any change or movement in your exterior life, in your physical universe. An event can be anything that somebody says or does, the arrival or the loss of anything from your life, as well as any ongoing situation or circumstance. Some events are trigger events that activate MODs.

Trigger event, or just "trigger": Any event (negative = "bad" in opinions of the activated person) that sparks a MOD by activating a NEIR mass to spring from the subconscious into consciousness-experience. The MOD activation is experienced primarily as neg-emo=UPS, but the NEIR is always there.

Game: All effort and struggle to overcome obstacles (to reach a goal). The essence of a Game, the great majority of the time and the experience, is in the struggle, not the goal. The purpose of a Game is to savor the struggle and the resulting Drama. The purpose of your entire human incarnation is to play the Human Game and so explore and savor Drama and UPS. In your Essence, you are too Wise and Powerful to play Games; you must counter-create your Essence with negative identities.

Drama: All the varied and rich experience, mostly negative, that we savor during the battle with problems and obstacles that is a Game. Drama includes all the negative emotions. Drama includes effort, struggle, problems, conflicts, uncertainty, doubt, suspense, frustration, impotence, impatience, anxiety, fear, anger, rage, desperation, depression, allies against enemies, losing and winning, victory and defeat, failure, sadness and sorrow, elation and despair, regret, guilt, giving up or perseverance, allies and enemies, etc.: a great variety of tasty experiences. Note that Drama is primarily negative experience, ergo UPS.

Game Conditions: To keep a Game and therefore its Drama going by not winning the Game. Most humans are in

Game Conditions → No Results → Drama and UPS

most of the time. You create and maintain yourself in Game Conditions by counter-creating your innate spiritual creator power. Your creator power and how you counter-create it we will see in Book 2.

DUPS: Abbreviation for Drama, Unhappiness, Pain, and Suffering. Drama is mostly negative experience and includes all the negative emotions; it is therefore mostly UPS.

Results: Results is achieving one's goals; getting whatever a person is trying to manifest in his experience, psycanic or physical. Results are Game Over and therefore End of Drama. No results maintain Game Conditions→Drama. Producing your desired results leads to a life of ease and satisfaction instead of DUPS. In all Games, you-human believe you are playing for results,

In life, you can have Drama or you can have Results, but never both. __The default choice of the UHB is Drama.__ You-psycan arrive to this reality programmed to maintain Game Conditions and create Drama. (This programming in in your Shell.) To change your life to Results, you must decide to do so and learn how, which is what psycanics teaches.

Power, personal power: Your ability to produce your desired results in any Arena of life. Most humans have their power suppressed to maintain Game Conditions and Drama. Too much power and you cannot play Games; you would overcome the obstacle and produce your desired result too easily and quickly.

Remember: when in doubt about a word, check the glossary. And the glossary is a fascinating read in itself.

6- Your Six Arenas of Experience

To the ordinary person living in the universal human condition of Drama and UPS, his internal world appears to be random, chaotic, and beyond control. However, that is not the nature of our interior life per se, but rather lack of understanding of how it operates.

Just as the external, physical universe operates "scientifically", that is by **cause→effect** and by laws and principles; so too does your internal world of emotions, thoughts, and relationships operate. Everything in your psycanic experience, whether Happiness or DUPS, is **cause→effect**. Your internal world is as fine a mechanism as any computer. If your computer is not producing your desired results, you know there is a problem with the hardware or the software. In the same way, if your life is not to your liking, if it is problematic, unhappy, even painful; it is because you have errors in the software with which you are operating it. All psycanic experience is the effect of psycanic energies on your consciousness. You can control those energies.

The Six Arenas (TT) of Life

Everything in your life falls into one of the Six Arenas of Experience; the Six Arenas of Life.

Each Arena comprises a different kind of energy. Think of your life as a circus, but instead of three rings, there are five: your life is a five-ring circus. Everything in your life occurs in one of these six areas, six Arenas.

The Six Arenas of Life are:

BE, FEEL, THINK, RELATE & DO, HAVE.

Synonyms for each Arena are:

Identities, Emotions, Mind, Relationships & Behaviors, Results.

Illustration: The Six Arenas of Human Experience

RELDO is the acronym for RELATE and DO, explained below.

The first four Arenas: BE, FEEL, THINK, and RELATE are **trans-physical =psycanic** energies that you-psycan experience "internally", directly in your consciousness (as opposed to "external" physical experience that comes through your body). They are trans-physical because you cannot capture, measure, or detect them (your BEing, emotions, thoughts, and relationship energies) with physical instruments. These first four realms of energies do not come from the physical universe or your body. Your psycanic (trans-physical) experiences occur directly to you-psycan, to your consciousness. (Consciousness, remember, is your power to experience; to perceive and feel energies-realities, both psycanic and physical.)

Your trans-physical experiences include:

➢ your identities = BEing (which produce your self-image and self-esteem),

➢ your emotions = FEELings,

➢ your thoughts = THINKing (everything in your mind), and

➢ your RELATE-ing, all relationship energies (communication, harmony and love, or problems and conflicts).

We will call all these your **psycanic** energies and your **psycanic** experience, to distinguish them from your physical experiences of the external world that you perceive through the five senses of your body.

Note on relationships: Bodies, hugs, sex, etc. are physical, but your relationships with others are psycanic in nature. Examples include: liking and disliking, paying attention or ignoring, acceptance or rejection, communication, harmony or disharmony, support or sabotage, love, anger, or hate. All these are trans-physical energies-experiences in the relationship. Thus, we consider **relationships psycanic rather than physical.**

Definition: Psycanic: all forms of energy→experiences that you-aware-will perceive directly in your consciousness. They do not come from the physical universe nor through the body; they are higher dimension of energy. Your psycanic energies include your identities, your emotions and feelings, all forms of thought, everything in your mind and memory, and the content and meaning of your communications, and your non-physical experiences of others in your relationships.

Illustration: Your Four Arenas of Psycanic Experience and
Two Arenas of Physical Experience
(separating RELATE and DO into two arenas).

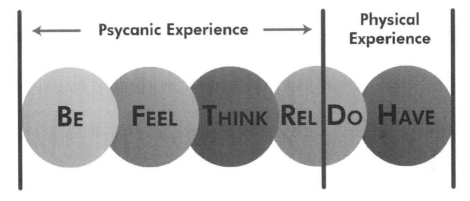

There is nothing random or accidental about your experience in each Arena; they all work according to laws and principles. Physics is the laws of the physical universe (FU); psycanics the laws of your psycanic universe (PU) Each Arena is a polarity; each Arena has positive experiences and negative experiences. Our purpose is to teach you how to control your experience in four Arenas of your PU (Psycanic Universe).

All your psycanic experiences are your creations. The external, physical universe has no power to create anything in your internal, psycanic universe. What you have created, you can discreate. You-psycan **can eliminate any negative experience in your interior life.** Being Transformation Technology (BTT) is a precision procedure for doing so.

An Introduction to Each Arena

Your **HAVE** is all your results in the material world:

➢ Body and health

➢ Career or business

➢ Money, investments, finances

➢ Home and properties

➢ Vehicles and other assets

➢ Clothes, tools, jewelry, etc.

Of particular interest are:

1- Negative HAVE: What you HAVE that you do not want but have not been able to eliminate (such as debts, health problems, overweight, a job you hate, a relationship you want to leave).

2- Desired HAVE: What you want but have not been able to manifest, such as a relationship or spouse, better job, more money, travel, more free time, move to a better neighborhood, etc.

— — — — — — — — — — — — —

Your DO is all your actions and behaviors. Examples of DO include:

Positive DO:

➢ Job performance and productivity

➢ Keeping your word

➢ Being on time

➢ Listening attentively

➢ Taking care of your family

➢ Lovemaking and sex

➢ Exercising regularly

➢ Honesty

Negative DO:

➢ Irresponsibility

➢ Laziness, postponement

➢ Addictions (alcohol, tobacco, drugs, gambling, sex, porn, shopping, etc.)

➢ Not exercising

➢ Overeating, eating junk food

➢ Not keeping your word

➢ Impunctuality

- ➢ All other things that you know are bad for you or for others, especially those that you have not been able to stop DOing: compulsions, obsessions, and addictions.
- ➢ All the things that you would like to DO but you have resistance or block to DOing (speaking in public, change jobs, divorce, start a business, writer's block, etc.)

— — — — — — — — — — —

Your RELATE

RELATE is a special case of DO. Your RELATE is all your DOings as regards other people, your behaviors in your relationships. Your RELATE includes:

1. What you say and how you say it;
2. How you deal with and treat others: with positive energy (love) or negative energy (anti-love); and
3. How you either respond positively (lovingly) or react negatively (anti-lovingly) to their treatment of you, particularly when they treat you with neg-energy.

Your positive RELATE includes: attentive listening (without judgments), precise communication, patience, serenity, understanding, caring, consideration, all of which are forms of love.

Your negative RELATE includes: invalidating others, criticizing, judging, nagging, not keeping your word, getting angry, withdrawal, the silent treatment, or otherwise punishing them. Neg-RELATE includes trying to control or to manipulate others, which includes guilting them (make them feel guilty so they do what you want). All of these are forms of neg-love, aka anti-love.

Your RELATE determines the quality of your relationships. If you use negative energy of any kind, *no matter your excuse,* **expect negative energy from the other person.**

Law of Love:

**If you wish to achieve True Happiness,
giving negative energy is NEVER justified.**

Law of Relationships:

**Don't expect the other person to change until you do,
and then you won't need the other person to change at all.**

**Others will usually change when you do because
you have changed the energy dynamics of the relationship.**

If you need the other person to change to improve the relationship or to be happier you are ignorant of how love, happiness, and relationships work. True Happiness is impervious to external events and needs nothing from others. It is neither affected by the behaviors or others nor has any programs and demands about how they should be.

Your THINK

Your life Arena of THINK is everything that occurs in your mind. Your THINKing includes your ideas, concepts, desires, goals, plans, dreams, memories, opinions, knowledge, learnings, intelligence, values, beliefs, dogmas, programs, paradigms, visions, imagination, creativity - to name a few.

As in all Arenas, your THINKing can be positive or negative.

Your mind is complex and requires, not a chapter, but its own book to explain how it works. In this book, we will cover only the few aspects of your mind that are critical to your power to discreate realities.

NOTE: THINK, RELATE, DO, and HAVE are explained in Book 3. There is simply too much information to fit in this Book 1 or Book 2. This Book 1 covers BE and FEEL only, and the discreation of NEIRs; what you need to get started in transforming your life with the Being Transformation Technology

Your FEEL

Your Arena of FEELing is all your emotions, both positive and negative.

- Positive FEEL includes all the positive emotions: peace, serenity, attraction, interest, contentment, satisfaction, interest, enthusiasm, delight, joy and ecstasy, to name a few. Your positive emotions are the only happiness that exists.

- Your negative FEEL includes ALL the negative, unpleasant, or painful emotions. The negative emotions include: aversion, anger, fear, anxiety, worry, guilt, regret, resentment, hate, sadness, sorrow, grief, boredom, apathy, emptiness, and depression - among others. It is UPS, the UPS that exists.

Something that I will repeat throughout this book: Your UPS is never what happens, but how you FEEL about what happens, your emotions. You will never always be able to control what happens; you can always control how you FEEL about it. This you do by eliminating all your negative emotions and creating permanent positive ones – and that is all that is necessary for True Happiness.

Law of Happiness

Your ONLY Happiness◇Unhappiness in life
is your own emotions.

Your UPS (Unhappiness, Pain, Suffering) in life is NEVER
what happens, but how you FEEL in relation to what happens.

The secret to True Happiness all the time no matter what is to control your emotions. Controlling the external world of events, including what others say and do, is impossible. With BTT, you can discreate all your negative emotions, energize and make strong and permanent your positive ones, and so achieve True Happiness. All this is explained in the video course on True Happiness.

We will have more to say about FEELing, about your emotions, in its chapter.

Your BEing

Your BEing comprises all that you are BEing (which is also delimited by all that you are not-BEing). **Your BEing is the sum total of your identities.** Your identities are your declarations, creations, of Self; of what you are and what you are not. There are only four important areas of identities: Wisdom, Power, Value, and Love-Joy (abbreviated WPVLJ).

As with all the Arenas of the Causal Sequence, identities and BEing are polarities. Your positive identities affirm your Wisdom (intelligence), Power to produce your desired results, your self-Value, and your Lovability (WPVLJ).

Your negative identities counter-create your WPVLJ (Wisdom, Power, Value, Love-Joy). Your negative BEing which comprises your negative WPVLJ identities are the root cause of all your difficulties and UPS in life. You are the creator of your negative IDs-BEing-Self; what you have created you can discreate. And that is our objective with BTT: that you learn to discreate your negative identities and so transform your BEing from negative to positive. This will transform your life.

Examples of your identity polarities are your creations of self such as:
"I am intelligent ◇ I am not intelligent."
"I am able ◇ I am unable." I am strong ◇ I am weak."
"I am a success ◇ I am a failure."
"I am worthy ◇ I am unworthy."
"I am a good ◇ I am a bad person /parent / spouse / daughter, etc."

Your identities may appear to be mere thoughts or beliefs, but not so. **Your negative identities are great masses of energy in your subconscious** that require hours of psycanic energy processing, of Being Transformation Technology, to discreate completely. They are not thoughts or beliefs you can simply change at will, nor cover over with affirmations.

We have an entire chapter coming on identities.

To close this chapter: Can you think of anything in your human experience that does not fall into one of the Six Arenas.?

7- The Causal Sequence

Here is where the magic begins.

The Six Arenas of Life (BE, FEEL, THINK, RELATE & DO, HAVE) are not independent, much less random. On the contrary, they exist and operate in an exact order, one of Cause→Effects.

The Six Arenas form the:

CAUSAL SEQUENCE of LIFE:

BE → FEEL → THINK→ RELATE & DO → HAVE

These are equivalent to:

IDentities → Emotions → Mind → Behaviors & Actions → Results

Causal Sequence of Life

BE → FEEL → THINK → RELDO → HAVE

Rel-Do= Relate & Do

Synonyms:

Identities → Emotions → Mind → Actions → Results

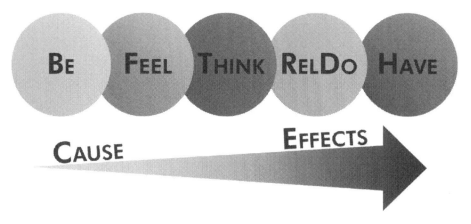

The abbreviation for the Causal Sequence is: BFTRDH

They are a *causal* sequence because **the elements to the left determine the elements to the right** (as indicated by the arrow).

Note: For clarity, we will use all capital letters when referring to any element of the Causal Sequence; e.g. BE, BEing; HAVE, HAVEing; FEELing; etc.

Your life consists of Causal Sequences.

Each situation in your life has its Causal Sequence and it always initiates in your identity, in your state of BEing. The secret to power over your life is that you can change your BEing and that will automatically change all the other elements in that causal Sequence.

Example of a Causal Sequence: Relationships: each interaction in a relationship is a Causal Sequence. If you are HAVEing negative results in a relationship (i.e. problems, conflicts), then you have a Causal Sequence something like this:

BE: You are (unconsciously) operating in a negative state of BEing, a negative identity. *(This is what you are learning to find in your subconscious and change.)*

FEEL: That neg-identity is generating your negative FEEL, negative emotions (i.e. frustration, anger, etc.). *ALL your neg-emotions come from your neg identities, no exceptions.*

THINK: You are creating some negative thoughts (aware of it or not) such as invalidating the other person, THINKing you are right and they are wrong; they are to blame; they must change. You have them as the "bad guys" of your relationship movie.

RELATE and DO: As you THINK they are the "bad" cause of the problem, you attack them overtly or subtlety with negative energy (such as anger, criticism, recriminations) in how you communicate and how you treat them. You say negative things; you argue; you try to control and change them, which is always anti-love.

HAVE: All this produces your negative RESULTS, your negative HAVE, of problems and conflicts in the relationship. Naturally, the other person resists your negative energy, defend themselves and counterattack you with their neg-love energies. Your results, your HAVE, is a poor quality relationship.

To see this, ask yourself: Where in my life are others attacking me with negative energy? However, the answer is not important. What is important is are you responding with love or with anti-love (neg-energy)?

What is important is: Where am I attacking others with negative energy, treating them with anything less than love, patience, understanding, acknowledgement, encouragement and gratitude? Who Am I that I am behaving so anti-lovingly? You can then trace your negative DO back to your negative causal identity, change it to positive, upon which you will cease to treat them negatively.

> Definitions: Love for others is what you DO, how you treat them; NOT what you feel. Love is a polarity. (Positive) love is all forms of positive energy. Neg-love, aka anti-love, is all forms of negative energy.

> Law of Love: Neg-love is NEVER justified. Love never uses neg-energy; it would not be love if it did so.

> Who do you profess to love, but you use neg-energy on them or treat them with neg-energy of any kind? --such as anger, invalidation, demands, expectations, intents to control, withdrawal of approval, affections, support.

All your relationship problems originate in your negative identities. Change your identity and entire Sequence changes. This brings us to the most important understanding about the Causal Sequence and your life:

You-the-BEing (psycan) are the ONLY causal element in your Causal Sequences, in your life.

You-spirit are the only thing alive; the only thing that has will and consciousness. You-psycan, the non-physical, aware-will entity, the BEing, are the only element that decides, and that moves (and experiences) energy. You are the only agent, the only element that can control your psycanic energies (mind, emotions, and identities). You-psycan are the causal element that moves your body, and through your body, moves your external, material world. You are the creator of your life, consciously or unconsciously. You are studying psycanics to make the process conscious so that you can take control of it. As long as it is subconscious, you will be creating mostly Drama and UPS instead of your desired results and True Happiness.

All the other elements of the Causal Sequence (emotions, thoughts, actions, material things) are lifeless things; they are energies, actions, or objects. You the BEing are the only power element in the Sequence. All the other elements are results of you-the-BEing creating thoughts and emotions, making decisions, taking action, and reaping the results. You are CAUSE, your other Arenas are all EFFECTs.

You-psycan create the (psycanic) realities, that then create your behaviors, relationships, and everything in your physical life. You make your creations unconscious to avoid results, maintain Game Conditions, and enjoy your Drama. This is not Bad-SNB: it is all planned.

Your fundamental error in life as a human is that you are trying to control and change the external world (FU) to change your internal world, to control your BE-FEEL, to stop your UPS and achieve happiness (PU). You are trying to THINK→RELATE / DO →HAVE to change your BE-FEEL. <u>You are trying to change your HAVE to change your BE.</u> (Your HAVE include others in your life, your relationships.) **This is the Causal Sequence in reverse: does not work. This, the External Quest, is impossible of success – and a therefore a grand generator of Drama.**

This great error, the External Quest, is fine while Drama is your goal in life. (Remember: the subconscious intention of every UHB is Drama; we-psycans all come to the Human Adventure Movie for the Drama.) If you want Power→Results→Satisfaction→Happiness, you need an entirely different strategy: control your BEing. Your BEing determines all the rest of your Causal Sequences.

You are creating your life now unconsciously. Psycanics will show you **<u>how</u>** you are creating your life so that you can take conscious control of the process and begin to create what you desire. The most important creation in your life is that of your own BEing: all else in your life flows out from that.

**Change your IDentities to change your BEing
and that Causal Sequence in your life
will change automatically.**

— —

Formulas:

**Psycan = spirit with power to take on any identity.
BEing: the net sum of all identities.**

**Psycan + Identities = BEing
(All that the psycan is BEing<>Not-BEing).**

Psycan + Human Identity Complex + Body = Human Being

Your Human Identity Complex (HIC) is a vast Shell, a Cocoon, of energy around you-psycan-consciousness that acts upon you-consciousness to generate your experience-illusion of BEing only a human being. Your HIC contains your personality, character, gender, talents, and all the distinct elements that make you a unique human being. It also contains all your negative identities, emotions and behaviors. With psycanics, you are learning how to go into this Shell and create and discreate its contents, its realities, and so to transform your life.

**The Magic of the Causal Sequence is that by controlling
your BEing, you automatically control all the other Arenas.
(FEEL, THINK, RELATE, DO, and HAVE).**

**Your control your BEing by discreating your
NEIRs (negative Essence identities) and creating
PEIRs (positive Essence identities.**

8 - The Schematic of Your BEing

The illustration, subject of this chapter, is a schematic, a blueprint, an x-ray, of your BEing. You are a multi-dimensional creature, a marvel of Divine engineering.

Your BEing includes:

#1- Essence, the One Creator BEing. From Her, you individualize BEcoming an (apparently) separate entity, a spirit. She has 13 Prime Characteristics: Oneness-Unity, Infinity, Light, Consciousness, Wisdom, Will (Power), Perfection, Beauty, Magnificence, Love, Peace, Joy, and Truth. You are made of Essence; we all are; all things are. The entire Creation is Essence in manifestation of Her Self. Beyond the illusion of isolated individuality we enjoy in the Creation, in our Matrix, we are all ONE.

#2 - You-psycan, the trans-physical=spirit-ual, life-energy entity, the spirit, that results from your individualization from the One. You "inherit" from Essence, your spiritual essence of BEing, your psycanic nature of WPVLJ: Consciousness, Will, Wisdom, Power, Value, and Love-Joy. (These are the four Characteristics of Essence that most affect you as a human being.)

- Your consciousness is your power to perceive energy-realities, to feel, to experience, to know.

- Your will is your power to move energy and so form realities, ergo to create and manifest what you want in life.

To become human, you must block and counter-create your Essence and psycanic nature as a spiritual BEing. Essentiality guides the person desiring to do so to discreate those blocks to re-establish experience of and communication with Essence.

#3 - Your Human Identity Complex (HIC): a vast Shell of trans-physical energies-realities, mostly subconscious, that encases you-psycan and acts upon you-consciousness to produce your experience of being a human being. It blocks out your awareness of your Self as spirit and your connections with Essence. It generates for you your unique human character and personality and everything else human about you. It contains your human memories and all aberrations and traumas. You-psycan can create and discreate realities in your HIC; you can re-create your human identity.

#4- Your HIC contains your NEIR Masses: specific identities that counter-create your WPVLJ (your wisdom, power, value and goodness) so that you can live in Game Conditions, explore Drama and UPS, and **all that you are not in Essence.** As a human being, you are exploring BEing the opposite of Essence. Your NEIR Masses get triggered into your consciousness-experience producing your MODs, negative results, problems, conflicts, and UPS in life. This book is primarily about the DISCREATION OF YOUR NEIR MASSES which will free your BEing from those counter-creations to your Essence and restore your divine Creator Power with which you can transform your life.

#5- Your body. Your body is your physical instrument and vehicle so that you-spirit can operate in, experience, travel in, and manipulate the FU (the "Fisical" Universe) as contrasted with your PU, your Psycanic Universe of all your trans-physical energies: mind, emotions, identities, relationships, etc.

YOU ARE NOT YOUR BODY. You HAVE a body. The body dies. YOU ARE NOT YOUR HUMAN IDENTITY. On death of your body, your Human Identity Complex (HIC, aka avatar) dissipates; you create a new one for your next incarnation. You are a psycan; an illusory individualization of the One Essence BEing. You-psycan are immortal, whether you choose to maintain your illusion of separate individuality from the One, or you choose to re-integrate and BE the One again (as did Jesus and Buddha). (Perception, communication and re-connection with the One Essence of All That Is, is the province of Essentiality, not psycanics.)

Throughout the book, we will be explaining the following diagram, your BEing, part by part; and teaching you how to take control of it and therefore of your life. We will be addressing your NEIR masses and their discreation. That is the key to great and quick change in your BEing and therefore in your life.

ESSENCE = WPVLJ
CREATOR AND SUBSTANCE OF ALL THAT IS

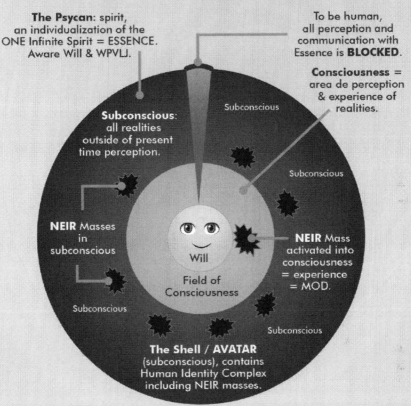

The Psycan: spirit, an individualization of the ONE Infinite Spirit = ESSENCE. Aware Will & WPVLJ.

To be human, all perception and communication with Essence is **BLOCKED**.

Consciousness = area de perception & experience of realities.

Subconscious: all realities outside of present time perception.

Subconscious

Subconscious

NEIR Masses in subconscious

NEIR Mass activated into consciousness = experience = MOD.

Will

Field of Consciousness

Subconscious

Subconscious

The Shell / AVATAR (subconscious), contains Human Identity Complex including NEIR masses.

The Human Body: vehicle and instrument for psycan operating on Earth.

The brain is organ of transduction between FU and PU energies. Sends perceptions "up" to psycan and receives "down" control.

9- The Causal Sequence Chart

All your negative emotions (FEEL), negative thoughts (THINK), negative energies and problems in relationships (RELATE), negative behaviors (DO) (such as addictions), and difficulties in manifesting what you want to HAVE in the physical universe are emanating from your negative BEing. Your negative BEing consists primarily of your negative Essence identities, NEIRs (later chapter).

Our objective is to identity the negative State of BEing (Identity / NEIR) that is the causal element in any negative experience or behavior (FEEL, THINK, RELATE, DO, HAVE. We then discreate the neg-ID and re-create ourselves in PEIRs.

The Causal Sequence Chart is a form that the explorer fills out to help him trace any negative experience or behavior in any of the 5 Arenas (FEEL, THINK, RELATE / DO, and HAVE) back to the causal NEIR, the causal state of BEing.

(You will probably need the guidance of a pilot the first few times until you get the hang of it. This support is you will find in the online Book 1 Support Groups to which you can enroll after taking the Psycanics BTT Course.)

Your objective is to learn to:

1. Take any negative experience or behavior in any of the 4 Effect Arenas (THINK, RELATE, DO, HAVE) and

2. Identify in experience your negative emotions (FEEL) you are trying to change with your negative THINK and DO; then

3. Penetrate the neg-emo to find your causal NEIR.

4. Discreate the NEIR (Negative Essence Identity Reality).

5. Re-create and energize your Self / BEing in PEIRs (Positive Essence Identity Realities).

6. Envision and energize the positive results you desire in each Arena upon which they will naturally manifest in your life.

For example: All your negative DO (e.g. addictions, compulsions, laziness, irresponsibility, no-action, etc.) are External Quest to avoid feeling your NEIR masses which contain all your negative emotions. All this we will see in Book III.

Example #2: All your negative RELATE are Don Quixote behaviors wherewith you are trying to change others to control your BE-FEEL, usually of anti-value. (Naturally, they resist your imposition and react with negative energy against you.)

In this Book I, we are will be tracing only your FEEL to your BE, learning to penetrate your neg-emo to find the NEIR and to discreate it. In Book III, we will study the rest of the Causal Sequence; how to trace anything in your THINK, RELATE, DO, and HAVE to the negative emotions you are trying to avoid and thence to the NEIR. (There is simply too much information for one book.) As always, discreate the causal NEIR and the entire Causal sequence will change.

How to Use the Chart

A MOD is a Moment of Dolor (Dolor is Latin for pain). A MOD is an activation into your experience (feeling) of a NEIR Mass. Your NEIR Masses are the source of all your negative emotions. Your NEIR Masses are **energy-reality-masses** of negative identities and emotions that reside in your subconscious, out of your perception-experience. Any negative event in your life can trigger a NEIR mass to jump from your subconscious to your consciousness-experience. You experience the activation primarily as negative emotions, ergo "Moment of Dolor"; but the NEIRs are always there inside the neg-emo. A synonym for a MOD is "activation".

A **NEIR mass** is a mass of psycanic energy consisting of a NEIR and its corresponding neg-emotions. You have many of these in your subconscious, created mostly in your childhood. When you experience a trigger event, that NEIR mass (ID + neg-emo) moves faster than the speed of thought from your subconscious to your consciousness-experience. You experience the NEIR mass primarily as neg-emo, as UPS. All this we will cover in great detail in coming chapters because your understanding of this is absolutely critical for your happiness.

Take the MOD activation, the negative emotion, you want to eliminate. Write it in the Negative FEEL box of the Chart. The Five Families of emotion are: anger, fear, sadness, guilt, and depression; note whichever best describes your FEELings.

Write in the **Trigger Event**. What is the event (any person, situation, thing) in your life that is triggering your MODs. Using the Arena of RELATE as example: a common example is what someone in your family does or says that you don't like, about which you activate.

Find your NEIR in experience (never in mind). For this Book I, we are interested that you find, in your experience, your NEIR. Who are you that FEEL as you do? You can use the emotion-NEIR correspondence table below to point you in the right direction, but you must find the NEIR in your experience.

Emotion-NEIR correspondence table

1. Anger: Present Time Anti-Power: I can't do/get (whatever).

2. Fear: Future Time Anti-Power: I am not going to be able to handle, control, stop, avoid, remedy (whatever).

3. Sadness: usually Anti-Value: Any form of expression of low self-value such as: I am not valuable; I am not good enough; I am unworthy; I am unloved; I don't deserve (whatever).

4. Guilt: Always: I am a bad person (for whatever reason).

5. Depression: Forever Anti-Power: I can't and I will never be able to. Helplessness + Hopelessness.

Once you have your NEIR in experience, you will discreate it with BTT and then re-create and energize PEIRs, positive identities.

This is all that you need to be able to do for Book I: trace neg-FEEL to neg-BE and discreate the neg-BE. Everything in Book III is about how to trace anything in the other 4 Arenas to your neg BE-FEEL where you will handle it as explained above.

CAUSAL SEQUENCE CHART

#4 Create PEIRs — Your PEIR ID will naturally manifest your desired results in the 4 Effects Arenas.

PEIRs	BE Identities	FEEL Emotions	THINK Mind	RELATE & DO Actions & Behaviors	HAVE Results
NEIRs		Neg-emotions (Anger, fear, sadness, guilt, depression, etc.)	Neg-thinking Bad-SNB Programs Demands	Neg behaviors What you do in your neg-energy relationships.	Neg HAVE A- What you HAVE that you don't want. B- What you want you don't HAVE.

#1

#2 Trace negs in any of these 4 Effect Arenas to the Causal NEIR

#3 Discreate NEIR

#4 Positive Experience to be manifested

#3 Negative Experience to be eliminated

Trigger Event:

Although we don't cover the 4 Effect Arenas of THINK, RELATE, DO, HAVE, until Book III, let's see if you can identity some of your energies and behaviors in them with this short discussion:

THINK:

1. Can you see that you are labeling Bad-SNB (bad, wrong, should not be doing that) something the other person says or does?

2. Can you see that you are extending that label of "bad" to the person, that you are making hir bad or wrong for doing what s/he is doing and so (apparently) causing your UPS?

3. Can you see that you have PROGRAMS (expectations, demands) about how the other person should BE or DO? Can you see you are trying to control or change the other person to stop them from activating your MODs, or to give you MOPs? Can you see that when they don't fulfill your programs (do what you want) you activate?

DO & RELATE:

Are you in any way attacking that person with neg-love (any form of neg-energy)? For examples: are you

- Spraying anger on them?

- Argue with them, even shout at them?

- Blaming and invalidating them for causing your MOD and UPS?

- Blaming them for anything else "bad" in your life? (You playing the Victim.)?

- Judging them, criticizing them?

- Disapproving of them, rejecting them?

- Trying to change them to not-do what triggers you, or to do something you want them to do? This is your Denial of Liberty to them to BE-DO as they think best for their happiness. It is pure egoism. It is your intent to dominate them and force them to sacrifice their happiness for yours. It is your Failure to Truly Love.

- Punishing them by withholding attention, approval, affection, communication, sex, or support?

All these are neg-love behaviors; anti-love. Anti-love is NEVER justified. As long as you are injecting any form and quantity of anti-love into your relationships, you can expect others to defend themselves from it, and to counter-attack to uphold their value (as "good" where you are labeling them "bad"). If you profess to love someone, are you treating them with neg-love;

are you anti-loving them? Remember the teachings of Jesus: Anti-love is NEVER justified, no matter what the other person does. There are powerful reasons why this law is so, to be found in Essentiality.

HAVE

Your negative HAVE in our example here of relationships will be problems, conflicts, and arguments with the person: i.e. a poor relationship, a negative relationship. In the block of HAVE, note down all the negative things in your relationship with that person. All of them are 100% your responsibility, not the other person's.

———————————————————————————————

In the Book I Online Support Group, you will list all the MODs you want to eliminate in your life. You will then do BTT on them under the guidance of the pilots in the online sessions. You will also learn much from seeing the problems and discreations of others (all is anonymous). You can eliminate the emotional charge on any trigger in an hour or two. If you persevere in discreating, you will eventually have discreated all your NEIR mass and be free of the negative human emotions, which is a condition necessary for True Happiness all the time, no matter what.

In Book III, you will learn to take any negative in any of the other Arenas (for example, an addiction) and trace it back to the Causal NEIR, where you will apply BTT to discreate it and re-create your Self in PEIRs.

10- PECRED

Essence, the Creator and the Substance of all creations, is static, the Unchanging, the Timeless. She is immovable, beyond all change. The Creation is always changing. In the Creation, change is the only constant. Change creates the illusion of time. Time can only be measured by movement, by change: time is change. If nothing changes, not even your thoughts, there would be no time.

The purpose of the entire Creation is to be a **field of realities producing experiences** of every kind possible. Each reality→experience is Essence taking that form to explore and experience Her Self in all Her infinite possibilities of BEing. You are not only one of those reality-experiences, you are also a sub-creator expanding the Creation from within; and you are a point of view, of experience, of the Creation from within. Everything you experience, Essence experiences through you.

The Creation is a **kaleidoscope** of energy→realities→experiences (ECRE), ever-changing. Old realities fade away (discreate) and new ones are always arising. You can take control of creation and discreation and accelerate them when you understand PECRED and ECRE (the center elements of P-ECRE-D). It is a major form of personal power to be able to discreate quickly your unwanted realities-experience.

PECRED and ECRE

PECRED is the acronym for the Sequence of Existence, which runs from Psycan to Discreation. The Sequence is:

Psycan (creator) → Energy → Creation → Reality → Experience → Discreation.

This is to be read and understood as:

The Psycan takes Energy and Creates his Realities, which then cause his Experiences, which then Discreate (on being fully experienced).

All the elements of PECRED operate according to laws and principles similar to those of physics and electronics in the physical universe – albeit with some critical differences.

ECRE

ECRE is the acronym for the middle four terms of PECRED:

Energy → Creations → Realities → Experience.

ECRE means and reads as:

Everything that exists is:

Energy formed **(Created)** into **Realities** which then cause **Experience =**

ECRE

ECRE refers to the masses of energy that are your realities and cause your experience. It is a more complete term for "realities" one that includes all the concepts involved: energy, creation, realities, and experience. All your psycanic experience is the impact of your ECRE on your consciousness. embodies the full nature of realities-experience. It's helpful to your understanding and creator power to think of all your realities (includes identities and NEIRs) as ECRE so that you apply all the characteristics and laws of each concept.

Explanation of Each Term in PECRED

Before we present some of the Laws of PECRED, we need to explain each concept:

Psycan

You are a spirit visiting Earth to enjoy the Human Adventure, play the Human Game, to star in your Human Movie. You are an immortal spiritual BEing formed of Essence; you are a "child" of the One Infinite Creator BEing, a "chip off the old block". In your spiritual nature, you have the same characteristics as Essence: Consciousness, Will, Wisdom, Power, Value, and Love-Joy. The acronym for these characteristics of BEing is: WPVLJ; you will see it frequently in psycanics because your WPVLJ identities are the most powerful identities in your life. You have counter-created your WPVLJ to be human. What we seek to do in psycanics is discreate your suppression of your WPVLJ so that you recover your Essence of BEing.

We call the spiritual entity of aware-will that you are a **psycan**. You-psycan are an individualization of Essence. You are incarnating inside the Creation to both experience it from your viewpoint, and to expand the Creation from within. You are a sub-creator, a co-creator of the universe. You expand the creation from within with all that you create in your life. You are also a sense organ, a point of experience for Essence: She experiences you (you are a creation of Essence) and then through you, everything that you experience.

You are as immortal as Essence; you are Essence; everything that exist is. As an individualization of the One Essence, you are a "child" of Essence and are playing in the Creation. At this moment in the eternity of your BEing, you are enjoying the Human Experience. **The Human Experience is the exploration of the negative side of the Creation**: anti-wisdom, anti-power, anti-value, and anti-love, and therefore of Drama and UPS. Just as you-human go to movies and enjoy sports for the Drama, so too do you-psycan-spirit come to Earth for the Human Game and all its Drama. Look at humanity and you can see billions of psycans incarnated in bodies and all spell-bound in their human identities savoring as much Drama as they can create.

The World Really Is The Matrix

You are an immortal spirit and the Creation is an illusion: Essence is the only Truth. The Creation comprises an infinity of planets, each a "movie theater" where psycan go to experience (The Purpose of the Creation and Life, remember, is Experience.).

Each theater is a Matrix (referring to the 1999 movie). Each Matrix is a creation, a simulation, a hologram, **but perfectly real** (as are all things created by God). Essence, individualized as we psycans, incarnates in the Matrices to experience that movie, to enjoy that adventure. Unlike human movies, **you don't watch divine movies: you live them; you star in them.** They are PERFECTLY REAL as only the Infinitely Powerful Creator can make them.

Earth is one such Matrix Theater. We-psycans incarnate on Earth for the Human Adventure, the Human Experience, to play the Human Game. The Human Matrix is about exploring negative experiences: Game Conditions (no power → not getting what you want), Drama, and UPS.

YOU ARE IN THE MATRIX.
To play in the Matrix and savor the illusion of being human,
YOU ARE ASLEEP to Who You Really Are,
a spirit-ual entity, part of the One Essence.

No matter what happens in the Human Matrix, it does not affect Who You Really are: Essence, the One, the Creator, aka God. You-psycan did not come here for all eternity. Eventually, after enough human incarnations, you will tire of the Human Drama and want to awaken from your Human Dream, remember and return to Who You Really Are. You do this by discreating the Shell of energy-realities around you-consciousness that generates for you the illusion of only being a human being. On freeing yourself of the Shell you return to BEing Essence (God) again. This is what Buddha and Jesus (and others) were teaching.

This awakening to your divinity and returning to the "kingdom of heaven", to perception and reconnection with the ONE, is core message of all religions. Essentiality is a technology of how achieve spiritual awakening, just as psycanics is a technology of how to control your human life. Students in the Essentiality School of Accelerated Enlightenment learn to perceive beyond their illusion of human being to recover and live in their experience of themselves as pure spirit and as creator of their lives.

There are two ways you can live life on Earth:

1- As a **UHB: Unenlightened Human Being**. A human being is a psycan (spirit) asleep to Who He Really Is, and so knows himself only as a human personality and a body. He is hypnotized and engrossed in his illusion of being only a human being. His life is centered in Games (problems and struggle for goals, ergo Drama and UPS (negative emotions). To play Games and have lots of Drama, you must **not-know** Who You Really Are. You must not-know that you are "Son of Essence, made in Her image and likeness": to wit a **Powerful Creator**. Were you to be powerful, you would produce your goals easily and quickly, and it would be **Game Over** and **End of Drama.** You are now faced with what to do to create more experience. To avoid this problem, we keep our Games going to suck all the Drama possible for as long as possible out of each one.

The vast majority of people on the planet right now are living as UHBs in Game Conditions (struggle) and DUPS (Drama and UPS). This is perfect: we-psycans all came here for the Human Adventure, for Games and DUPS. Thus, in playing the Human Game, all psycans/human beings are quite successful: we are all getting what we came here for: Games and DUPS.

None of this is accidental. Every Human Adventure is a creation of the psycan, *however unconscious the human identity is of it.* Creation must be subconscious to produce our desired results of NO-POWER, ergo Game Conditions and Drama. When you create unconsciously – as you do in your human identity-- you will create a lot of what you don't want, and fail to create a lot of what you do want – which is great DUPS. We will come back to this in the chapter on the Fatal Identity: your creation that you are not creator.

2- The second way that you can live life on Earth is as an **SEB: A Spiritually Enlightened Being**. An SEB is a psycan who has awakened to Who He Really Is: immortal spirit. He lives in the experience of being a trans-physical, spirit-ual BEing just visiting Earth and using a human identity and a body to play on Earth. He has recovered his perception, connection, and communication with the ONE.

He also recovers his awareness of his innate, divine power of creator. An SEB consciously CREATES his inner life, his BEing, emotions and thoughts. And he consciously CREATES his outer life: his relationships and his HAVE, his results, in the physical universe, results such as success and financial abundance.

I speak of all this not just theoretically but because I and dozens of other graduates of the Essentiality School of Accelerated Enlightenment have awakened and reached Enlightenment. We live able to perceive the ONE at will and consciously creating our lives. We have eliminated all Drama sand live in serenity, harmony, joy, and abundance.

This is not good or bad, better or worse, than UHB-Games-Drama-UPS. It is a question of what do **you** want to experience: Drama or Results, effort and struggle, or "easy street"? It is a matter of choice; of what you want in life. You can have whatever you choose, but not both. If you are reading this book, then some part of you is probably tired of DUPS and is seeking to create a happier life.

The point here is that **you are a CREATOR**, whether you acknowledge it or not, whether you want to be or not, whether you like it or not, whether you are conscious or unconscious of it. You can no more escape being creator than a tiger can escape his stripes. The question is **WHAT** are you creating? Game Conditions→DUPS, or Results→Satisfaction→Happiness?

You are creating all your experience, both psycanic and physical. **You are doing this consciously, or you are doing it unconsciously**. As long as you are doing it unconsciously, you will be a creating a lot of what you don't want and failing to create a lot of what you do want, which is Drama.

Again: Drama and UPS are not Bad-SNB; they are very rich experiences. It is a question of what you want. Human beings will usually emphatically deny that they want no-results and Drama; but the psycan does. You-psycan chose the Human Movie for the Drama. You decide when you have had enough Drama and want to recover your creator power and create a life of ease and abundance and happiness.

You need not believe or even understand any of the above: psycanics and discreation will work fine no matter what you believe you are, as long as you apply the Laws of PECRED (presented in a later chapter). You can put all we have said about Essence and spirit and psycan in Mu (TT), meaning to suspend belief *and* disbelief until you have proof one way or the other.

Creator of your Psycanic Experience

You-psycan are the creator of all your psycanic realities and therefore of all your psycanic experience. PECRED: You-psycan-will-power take energy and form it, create it, into your psycanic realities (such as identities, emotions, thoughts, behaviors). Those realities then produce your experience. As a human being, you do this unconsciously and so create many negative (undesired) things in your life producing Drama and UPS.

You are the Creator of your life.

You are a psycan, child of Essence.
You were created to create and experience.
(There is nothing else to do in the Creation.)

Everything in your life is your creation.
You-psycan are the soul and sole creator of your life.

You are the creator of all your experiences
including the experience that you are not the creator
of your experience when that is your experience.

Your life is your movie: you are the script writer,
the director, the star and the hero.

What you have created, you can discreate.

You are the creator of everything negative in your life: everything you don't want; everything you are trying to avoid or stop; everything that is UPS for you, including all your relationship problems and conflicts. You are also the creator of **not getting** what you want. And you are the creator of **not being able to eliminate** all that you do not want (for example, health problems, bad relationships, addictions, debts.).

Energy Energizes

This brings us to an important Law of Creation:

All energy energizes, irrelevant of the polarity.
To energize is to pour energy into a reality which increases its mass
and therefore its density (its capacity to cause experience) and
makes that reality more persistent.

The Law of Energy Energizes means that all the time you allow yourself to
stay in negative energy (for examples: aversion, resistance, anger, fear,
sorrow, guilt, depression, etc.), you are energizing→manifesting or persisting
something you don't want.

Law:

**All the time that you are in neg-energy (towards anything) you
are energizing and therefore manifesting or persisting what you
don't want.**

Another way to express this law is:

Resistance causes Persistence.
(All negative energy is resistance.)

Can you afford to let yourself remain in negative energies?
The price is anti-power (no results) and UPS.

Introduction to the Fatal Identity

It is also your creation that you are NOT the creator of the negative things in
your life, which is the Fatal Identity. The Fatal Identity initiates the Fatal
Identity Sequence. This consists of the Fatal Paradigm which triggers the
Impossible Dream of the External Quest. The External Quest includes the
Emotional Roller Coaster, the Merry-Go-Round for the Golden Ring of
Happiness, and the Don Quixote behaviors. All of these stop you from
achieving True Happiness; we will examine each in detail in a coming chapter.

The Law of the Fatal Identity.

The following law is one we will repeat in this book each time it is relevant:

**You-psycan are the creator of all your realities, including
the reality that you are not the creator of your realities,
when that is your reality --**
as it is for most UHBs.

Most human beings live in their ECRE (energy-creation-reality-experience) that they are NOT the creator of their experiences (The Fatal Identity Sequence). This illusion is great for producing Drama and counter-productive for Power, for producing your Desired Results.

We are here seeking to awaken you from the illusion of the Fatal Identity that you are NOT Creator. Only so awakened can you reclaim your Creator Power and re-create your BEing and your life as you would have it.

We will cover the Fatal Identity and its Sequence in detail in Book 2.

Your BEing

Your first and most important creation as a psycan is your creation of your BEing, the first element in your Causal Sequences. Your BEing is all that you are being, also defined by all that you are not-being (for example, creating that you are not creator). What you are Being and not-BEing is created, determined, by your identities. Your BEing comprises the totality of all your identities.

Your identities are individual creations of what you are, and what you are not. Your important identities are your Essence identities, those which affirm or deny your Wisdom, Power, Value, and Goodness-Love-ability. We will explain all this over several chapters.

Human Being

"Human being" is one of your creations of BEing. You-psycan are an immortal spirit playing at being human. You are a spirit enjoying the **illusion** of only being a human being, of being a human identity. You create your illusion of human being by creating a Shell* of ECRE around you called your Human Identity Complex (HIC). This Shell of ECRE acts upon you-consciousness to produce your experience (illusion) of your human identity. You create a new Shell, a new HIC (Human Identity Complex), for each incarnation and you-psycan have hundreds of human incarnations. *(We will cap "Shell" when referring to your human identity Shell to avoid any confusion with any other use of the word.)

Your "human being" is not alive! You-psycan are the only thing alive; you are consciousness and will. Your "human being" is a great structure, a great cloud of energy, a shell or cocoon of millions of realities, around you-consciousness. Think of your consciousness like the screen of a computer. What plays on the screen is experience. Your HIC is like the software in a computer; it determines what appears images and text that appear on the screen of your experience. Currently, your software is "human being".

To fully savor the Human Experience, you must **not-know** Who You Really Are and what you are truly capable of. To take your human adventure seriously, you must suppress your True Identity with your illusion of human being. As a human being, you are not-wise, not-powerful, not-valuable, and can be a "bad" (person). Thus, you can explore Game Conditions and Drama and UPS, things you cannot experience bb in Essence-WPVLJ.

As a human being, you are not supposed to know all this. You came to Earth to lose your Self in your human identity and live your human movie as a human, seriously and dramatically. You can recover your consciousness of Who You Really Are, restore your WPVLJ and live on Earth as an Awakened Spirit whenever you want.

Energy

The next term in PECRED is **Energy**: Psycan→ **Energy** → Creation→ Reality→ Experience→ Discreation.

1- **Everything that exists is formed of energy.** Every thing, every object, that exists in the Creation is energy taking that form. Einstein expressed this even for (apparently) solid matter with his famous equation: $E = mc^2$. Quantum mechanics confirms this noting that sub-atomic particles are patterns of energy, of vibrations in the quantum fields.

"Everything that exists" includes all your psycanic realities, your identities, thoughts and emotions. Your thoughts are energy forms; your emotions are charges of energy. Low self-esteem is a negative energy about your self-worth. Love is positive energy. Hate is negative energy. Your HIC Shell of human being is all energy. All your BE, FEEL, THINK, and RELATE are psycanic are energies (ECRE) that, when activated into your consciousness, produce your experience of them. IT IS ALL ENERGY, and all energy is ESSENCE in disguise, forming for us the playground of the universe so we can live human movies and adventures and explore Drama.

2- **All energy is legal. All energy, physical and psycanic, obeys exact laws and principles.** The laws that determine your identities and emotions, happiness and pain, are just as exact and powerful as the laws that hold the planets in their orbits. In the physical universe, the laws of energy comprise our physical sciences: physics, chemistry, thermodynamics, etc. We call the laws of energy (ECRE) in your internal universe "psycanics". Psycanics is the laws of the trans-physical energies of your experience in the Arenas of BE, FEEL, THINK, and RELATE. All your thoughts, emotions, behaviors, relationships, happiness◇UPS, and love◇anti-love are "lawful": they operate according to exact laws.

Nothing in your experience is accidental or random: everything is cause◇effect. Every negative emotion, all your UPS, has an exact cause in your psycanic world. You can control and eliminate those causes and thus eliminate all UPS. *(You are in the process of learning how.)*

All things are forms of energy, energy forms. All things are masses of energy being that thing; they are energy with a specific identity. We call all forms of energy "realities". A reality is energy being any particular thing. A reality is energy taking on an identity. If it exists, it is a reality. All your experience is energy in the form of realities, ECRE, acting upon you-consciousness. Realities Cause Experience; Experience is the Effect of Realities on consciousness.

Create and Creations

The next element of PECRED is **Creation**:

Psycan→ Energy→ **Creation**→ Reality→ Experience→ Discreation.

The psycan takes energy and forms, CREATES, his creations=**realities**.

Energy formed into a reality, into any thing or object, is a creation. All realities are creations. All realities were created by someone, somewhere, sometime. Nothing in the Creation has sprung into existence without being created; there is always a creator force. Again, the term "ECRE", (energy→ creation→ reality→ experience) reminds us that all the four concepts are intimately related.

The ultimate source of all that exists is Essence; She is both the Creator and the Substance (Energy) out of which everything is created. She manifests the Creation as a playground, as a Disneyland, as theaters, as Matrices for experience. However, you are the creator of your psycanic universe of realities-experience (identities, emotions, thoughts). You are also the creator of your human life. **Deny that you are the creator and you will have no power over your ECRE.** *We will come back to this in a later chapter as it is of extreme importance.*

To create is to cause a reality to exist. It is to use your will to move energy and form your desired reality. Think of a tree. Think of a house. You are forming mental energy into those images; you are creating those mental realities; and then you are experiencing them with your consciousness. You can create psycanically (thoughts, emotions) very quickly. Creation in the physical universe (from the human level of being) usually takes time and is often more a question of manifestation (attraction) than creation.

To manifest is to cause a reality already created, usually by someone else, to appear in your life, in your experience. You create a painting or a business. You manifest a spouse or a house. To manifest, you create the mental reality, the pattern, of what you desire, and you willfully energize that pattern reality over time with the intention that it come into your life.

If you were re-integrated completely to Essence, BEing Essence again, anything you willed would manifest instantly, as demonstrated by the Illuminati (Buddha, Jesus, Lao Tzu, etc.) *(The Illuminati are a group of about 235 Beings who not only awakened from the Human Dream but completely re-integrated with Essence such that they were the One walking the earth in a human body. (Thus, Jesus could say: "The Father and I are One.")* However, to BE a human being and explore Game Conditions and Drama, you counter-created your Essential Power so that manifestation is difficult, long, and iffy (often fails). This is because your experiential purpose in coming to the Human Experience is not Power and Results, but Game Conditions and Drama.

Psycanics contains processes to start the process of recovering your Creator Power. Graduates of psycanics experience a notable increase in their power to create and manifest in the physical universe. They live working only in their passions, with all their relationships in harmony, and manifest success and abundance easily. However, full recovery of your innate Divine Power requires advanced processes that are part of Essentiality.

Realities

The next term in PECRED is **Realities**:

The psycan takes **energy** and creates his **Realities** (which include identities).

A reality is any form or mass of energy; it is energy being some thing, an entity. A reality is energy taking on an identity. Everything that exists is a reality. The Creation consist of an infinity of realities of all kinds.

You have physical realities such as galaxies, stars, planets, trees, houses, rocks, animals, atoms, electrons. Notice how physical realities are modulated masses of energy. (Modulate is an electronics term meaning to give a particular wave form to energy; we use the term to mean to form energy in a particular way to create the desire reality-experience.)

You have your personal, psycanic realities such as thoughts, memories, mental images; and all the emotions (joy, anger, fear, hate, sorrow, loneliness, grief, guilt, regret, resentment, depression, etc. The most powerful of all your psycanic realities are your identities, your creations of what you are or are not.

Your psycanic realities are also masses and charges of energy. They impact you-consciousness causing you the perception and experience of that mass. When the energy in the mass is "loose" and ready to flow, to discharge, we say that it is a **charge**. For example, your negative emotions are **charges** of energy that flow, rush, into your consciousness producing your experience of that emotion.

Spiritual Realities

As a human being, you do not have much access to spiritual realities, such a perception and communication with Essence (who is WPVLJ: Wisdom, Power, Value, Love-Joy, and therefore happiness). But this is not because spiritual realities do not exist, but because you have blocked your perceptions to be able to live as a human being in **avidya** (avidya: meaning spiritual ignorance: a term in Hinduism and Buddhism referring to human condition of **not-knowing** Who You Are and where you come from (Essence). Avidya is essential to Drama; you cannot pretend and experience being a human if you are experiencing Who You Really Are, a powerful spiritual BEing, part of the All That Is.

You experience physical realities through your body and its five senses. Your brain (never to be confused with your mind) transduces the electrical signals from your organs of sight, sound, smell, touch, taste, to energies that act upon you-consciousness so that you perceive physical universe objects and energies (light, sound, heat, etc.).

You-psycan experience your **psycanic** realities, your identities (BE), emotion (FEEL), and thoughts (THINK) directly in consciousness. These do not come from the physical universe nor through your body and nervous system as do physical energies.

Reality and Experience are the two sides of the same coin.

Realities cause experience.
Experience is the effect of realities (on consciousness).

(**RExp** is the acronym for <u>R</u>eality-<u>E</u>xperience as one thing;
ECRE is the acronym for the complete concept.)

— —

You-psycan are the creator and discreator of your realities:
What you have created, you can discreate.

(Discreation is the opposite of creation which is to cause a reality to exist. Discreation is to terminate the existence of a reality.)

The Fatal Identity and Denial of Responsability (DOR) for a creation, makes it not-yours and kills your power to discreate.

DOR kills the power to discreate.

Experience Experienced Discreates (Exp2→0).
Resistance Causes Persistence (Rxx→Perxx).

Experience

The next term in PECRED is **Experience:**

The psycan takes energy and creates realities which he then **experiences.**

Experience is one of the most fundamental of all the concepts in Psycanics and Essentiality (which deals with how to recover your experience of Essence, of God). It is the very purpose of the Creation itself. As we have explained the concept of Experience in a previous chapter, there is no need to repeat it here.

— —

Discreation

The last term in PECRED is **Discreation:**

The psycan takes energy and creates realities which he then experiences, upon which they **Discreate** (cease to exist).

Law of PECRED: The purpose of the creation of a reality is experience. A reality persists until it has fulfilled its purpose, until it has been fully experienced, upon which it discreates making space for new realities–experiences. Thus does the Creation change, flowing from one state of existence to another, always renewing itself.

To discreate a reality is to discharge the energy from it (by experiencing it) so that that form, that mass of energy, that reality, no longer exists. What does not exist can no longer cause you experience, UPS. The fundamental law of discreation is:

Experienced Experience Discreates (abbreviated: Exp2 —>0).

We have here an opportunity to mention an important understanding that I will repeat multiple times in this book:

This experience of his experience, of his realities, is exactly what the human being (humbe) <u>does not do</u>; what you are not doing. The humbe <u>resists</u> his experience, his ECRE. He tries to avoid feeling his negative experience, to stop it, or block it, or suppress it. He does everything possible **NOT** to feel his negative ECRE. (One example: suppress negative feelings with chemicals such as alcohol, tobacco, tranquilizers, legal and illegal drugs (which creates addictions to those substances. You will learn how to cure addictions in Book III; BTT does so easily.

Resistance Causes Persistence of the ECRE being resisted.
Resistance is all forms of negation to experience, and all forms of neg-energy used to attack the negative reality.

Discharge of Energy and Discreation of Realities

All the time that you-psycan at Cause (in consciousness of creator and power) and are experiencing a reality (ECRE) without resistance, you are discharging the energy from it. Realities are masses of energy. Experience = discharge an ECRE enough, and there will be no energy left, therefore no more of that reality. It is like hooking up a battery to a light, where the battery represents the charge and the light your experience. If you keep the light on, eventually the battery energy will be exhausted.

We will come back to discreation in more detail in Section II of this book. For now, I trust that you understand the concepts that make up the acronyms of PECRED and ECRE. Their comprehension are building blocks in your personal power to create and discreate and so control your BEing. Control your BEing, re-create it positive, recover your WPVLJ and you will re-create your life. In the next two chapters, we are going more deeply into the nature of your BEing of the first and only powerful, creator element in your Causal Sequences, in your life.

11- BEing

BEing is a marvelous phenomenon which, once understood, can only leave you in awe of the Wisdom and Complexity of the Creator and Her Creation. Your BEing is also the most important of all your creations; which, as the initial element in the Causal Sequence, determines all the rest of your life.

You-psycan are a child of Essence-Creator. As such, you are innately a creator; you cannot not-BE a creator; you cannot not-create, no more than your body can stop breathing and live. Your purpose of existence is to play in the Creation, to create and expand the Creation, and to experience whatever you wish. Thus, one of your primary BEings is creator.

As a psycan, you are only Essence. To play in the Creation, you BEcome other things; these are your BEings, all that you are BEing defined also by all that you are Not-BEing. For example, if you create you are weak, you are not-BEing strong. You are Essence first BEing a psycan, and then BEing many other things, among them BEing a human being. As a human being, you must Not-BE Essence (WPVLJ) to create Game Conditions and DUPS.

You-psycan are currently creating BEing a human being and **not-BEing Essence, not-BEing WPVLJ** (Wisdom, Power, Value, Goodness/Love-Joy). To Not-BE WPVLJ, you have created a (illusory) BEing of anti-WPVLJ.

Your Being is composed of your identities, individual statements of BEing or Not-BEing. Your BEing is the sum of your identities. Your anti-WPVLJ BEing, which include human being, consists of many identities which deny your wisdom, intelligence, learning ability, knowledge, power, capability, strength, success, value, worthiness, deserving this, goodness, and lovability (being lovable).

As a humbe, you do not cease to create; you have only driven the process "underground", out of consciousness. Out of consciousness is out of control; thus you create many things you do not want (e.g. failure, relationship problems, health problems, etc.) which are all great Drama. You also fail to create many things you do want, also great Drama. You are also creating your negative identities, neg-emo, and all thoughts, your relationships, your successes and failures, your accidents and problems, and all your UPS. No matter what you are experiencing, you are creating it.

One of the secondary characteristics of Essence is Liberty, Freedom. As a "son of Essence" you are also totally free, and free to BE and to create anything you please. There are no Bad-SNB creations – this is impossible-- and Essence has absolutely no opinion or limitation on what you create. You are free to create Drama and UPS, success or failure, love or bigotry, even to BE→ DO evil. There are NO limitations whatsoever.

BEing is superior to all other creations. All other creations are subject to your creation of who you are BEing. When you are BEing anti-Essence by creating your anti-WPVLJ identities (NEIRs), you will not be able to (easily and quickly if at all) manifest anything that contradicts those identities-BEing; that violates Who You Are, by your own determination. With your anti-WPVLJ identities, you are declaring to the universe you are: ignorant, less intelligent than others, stupid, incapable, weak, a failure, less than others, undeserving, bad, unlovable, etc.

Does a BEing with those characteristics deserve to manifest easily and quickly positive things: a better job or a business, success, money, abundance, car, house, friends, spouse, etc.? No, not when such manifestations would contradict his BEing identities such as ignorant, stupid, unable, incapable, weak, less than others, undeserving, unworthy, bad person, etc. What he will manifest is a lot of struggle to achieve his goals (Game Conditions), poor results, Drama, and UPS – which is fine, that is why we are here.

Your BEing is your primordial creation and is superior to all other creations. **You can only manifest what agrees, goes, with your BEing.**

Where your identities→BEing is negative, you will create negative Causal Sequences: poor results, problems, conflicts → ergo, difficulties, errors, failures, ergo Drama and UPS. Again, all this is exactly as your planned BEing human. You created your anti-Essence identities = BEing precisely to create Game Conditions, Drama and UPS. Congratulate yourself on a job well done!

Change your identities➔ BEing to positive, and you will automatically create good results, abundance, and satisfaction. We want to make conscious how your BEing works so you can take control of re-creating it as you want and need it to BE to manifest the life you want. You change your BEing to positive by discreating all your anti-Essence identities (NEIRs) and re-creating your Self in positive Essence Identities, PEIRs, identities that affirm your Essence-WPVLJ. Your PEIR◇NEIR identities polarities are the very heart of psycanics and the principal target of BTT. We will come back to your PEIR◇NEIRs in few chapters.

We repeat the following from the previous chapter because it is a crucial understanding to your power over your life:

**You-psycan➔Being are the ONLY Causal Element
in your Causal Sequences = in your life.**

You-psycan-BEing are the only thing that has will and consciousness; the only thing that decides and experiences. Only you-psycan-BEing are creator; all else are your creations. Everything in your other four Arenas is either psycanic ECRE (your thoughts, emotions, relationships, behaviors); or physical matter (your HAVE). Your ECRE are lifeless realities; they are effects, results, of your BEing creating them.

You-psycan-BEing are the only power in your Causal Sequences, in your life. You are the only thing **that can move energy and therefore that can create and discreate.** (Creation and discreation are a matter of moving energy into and out of reality masses.) Your **energies=experiences** in all the other Arenas of Life are your creations, your results.

Control your BEing and your control your life
as it manifests according to the Causal Sequence

**Your BEing consists of identities that you can create and discreate
to transform your Self to BE the BEing you need to BE
to naturally manifest the life you want.**

**Your life will always be in accord with your BEing.
You cannot manifest anything in the FU that would
contradict your BEing.**

The Fatal Identity again

We need to mention here a primordial creation of BEing, of not-BEing creator. The UHB (Unenlightened Human Being) lives in his creation that he is **not** the creator of his life; that he lives in a dead, impersonal –or even hostile– universe over which he has little power and where he must struggle to survive and to get what he wants. This self-created illusion of powerlessness maintains Game Conditions, Drama and UPS, which, you remember, are the purpose of your Human Adventure Movie. You can choose to continue living in powerlessness and Drama, or you can Awaken to who you really are, recover your power and create your life as you would have it. This is "returning to the Garden of Eden". There is much more to the Fatal Identity Sequence that we shall see in its own chapter.

You have multiple levels of BEing:

1- **Essence**, the One Infinite Creator BEing who manifests all that exists out of Her own Essence / Energy.

2- **Psycan**: an individualization of Essence, with the same power of Consciousness and Creator. In your Essence, you are Consciousness, Wisdom, Power (Will), Value, and Love-Joy (WPVLJ). (Remember: Consciousness is the power to perceive and experience. Will is the power to move energy to form (create) realities/identities, or to discreate realities.) Your Essential nature you must counter-create to BE a human being. Relative to Essence=God, human beings are negative WPVJ: ignorant, stupid, powerless, neg-value, anti-love entities (anti-love entities: they generate lots of negative energy of all kinds).

3- **BEings**: you-psycan create your BEingnesses. Your BEings are what you-psycan are BEing (or Not-BEing) to assume a role and play in the Creation. You-psycan are currently BEing a human being, among many other things. (You have other kinds BEings that are the realm of Essentiality.)

   Identities: Your BEing is composed of your identities. These are your individual *creations→realities→experiences* (ECREs) of what you are and what you are not. The totality of your identities forms your BEing. (Chapter coming on identities.)

4- **Human being:** Your HIC (Human Identity Complex) is a shell of ECRE around you-psycan-consciousness-experience that generates for you your illusion of being a human being.

5- **Body:** Your physical body is not technically a BEing but rather an instrument and vehicle that you-psycan possess and use to operate in physical reality. However, many UHBs do firmly believe they are their body. You are not your body and to identify your Self as one is a low state of spiritual awareness.

Essence

What Essence is, and your relationship with Her, can be found in the Essentiality materials. You can download the free introductory book, *Essentiality I*, at www.Essentiality.org, or get the paperback at Amazon. You need not understand Essence or even psycan to acquire power over your life; but awakening to and experiencing Who You Really Are is the beginning of True Spirituality and the greatest wealth in life. True Spirituality begins when you *experience* that you are a spirit pretending to be human. When you live in that awareness, that experience, of being an immortal spirit all the time, you are Enlightened. You have transcended the illusion of human being. Enlightenment is the goal of Buddhism, Hinduism, and Taoism. In Christianity, it is poorly understood and is called the return to the "Garden of Paradise", or the "Kingdom of Heaven", also "salvation" and "redemption".

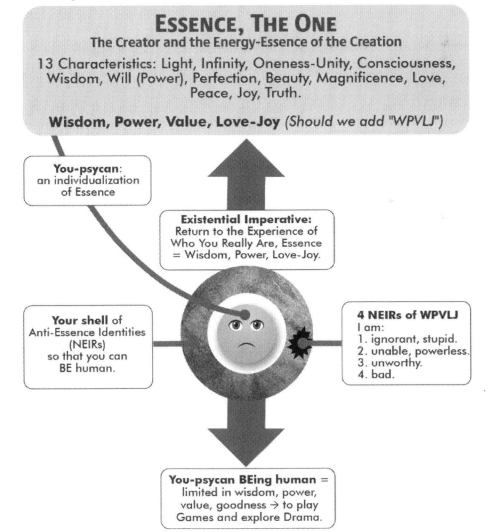

ESSENCE, THE ONE
The Creator and the Energy-Essence of the Creation
13 Characteristics: Light, Infinity, Oneness-Unity, Consciousness, Wisdom, Will (Power), Perfection, Beauty, Magnificence, Love, Peace, Joy, Truth.

Wisdom, Power, Value, Love-Joy (Should we add "WPVLJ")

You-psycan: an individualization of Essence

Existential Imperative: Return to the Experience of Who You Really Are, Essence = Wisdom, Power, Love-Joy.

Your shell of Anti-Essence Identities (NEIRs) so that you can BE human.

4 NEIRs of WPVLJ I am:
1. ignorant, stupid.
2. unable, powerless.
3. unworthy.
4. bad.

You-psycan BEing human = limited in wisdom, power, value, goodness → to play Games and explore Drama.

Psycan

You are an immortal, nonphysical (i.e. spiritual) life energy entity of will and consciousness, of aware-will. **There is only ONE INFINITE CONSCIOUSNESS.** You are self-created by individualizing your consciousness from the One Infinite Consciousness that is Creator of all that is. You-psycan are a "chip off the block" of Essence. You are offspring of the Creator, a child of God, with the same powers: the ability to create your realities→experiences (which includes your identities); to experience those creations and to discreate them.

Definition: **Psycan**: The **non-physical=spiritual** entity of Aware Will and WPVLJ that you are in your original and Essential nature. It is Who You Really Are before and beyond your creations of BEingnesses, particularly of human being.

Definitions: **Consciousness**: your consciousness is a field of super high-frequency life energy. It is your power to perceive and experience, starting with your Self, and your identities, then including your emotions and thoughts and relationships and ending with your experience of the physical universe through your five corporal senses.

Definition: **Will**: your will is your power to move and to form energy (into realities); it is your creator power. (Creation and discreation are processes of moving energy into or out of realities. Identities are one form of realities, thoughts and emotions are other forms.) You manifest what you want in the physical universe by mocking up the desired reality-experience in your psycanic universe and then energizing it, which attracts that reality into your life. When you are in your Essence, you have the same power to manifest as Jesus and Buddha: total power over the physical universe. However, as a human being you have blocked and counter created your Essence (WPVLJ) so you can BE human and explore the negative side of the Creation which includes Drama and UPS. Drama, you remember, is a condition of No-Power, ergo No-Results, ergo Game Conditions, ergo Drama.

BEing

As a psycan, a creator spirit, your foremost creation is your own BEing. Your BEing is all that you are BEing, also defined by all that you are Not-BEing. Then from your BEing, or through your BEing; you manifest all the rest of your life, your experiences in the Six Arenas of FEEL, THINK, RELATE, DO, HAVE. All the rest of your life will be in accordance with your BEing. It is a Law of Creation that you cannot manifest anything that would contradict your BEing. This is one of the reasons human beings find it so difficult to manifest all that they want.

For one example of BEing, you-psycan are currently BEing a human being so you can play the Human Game on Earth. You-psycan have created and are living as your total reality (the illusion of) BEing only a human being. You have blocked out your true spiritual nature so you can visit Earth and live a human life-experience. Right now, you are experiencing and are firmly convinced (by your Shell) that you are only a human being; you do not detect your true nature. That is fine; that is how you planned it for incarnating on Earth. But it is not the Ultimate Truth of Who You Are. You can choose to awaken from your Human Illusion to Who You Are, or to remain in your illusion of human.

Your Shell

You create your human BEing by creating a **Shell of ECRE, of realities and identities** around you-consciousness. That Shell or Cocoon acts upon you-psycan to produce your experience of **BEing** those identities, which include your NEIRs. You-psycan are **BEing** a human being. Your "human being" is a vast and complex structure of realities, a Shell of ECRE, that surround you-psycan and act upon you as consciousness to produce your experience of BEing only a human being. In turn, your human being comprises many identities, which are your individual creations of what you are and what you are not.

**You-psycan can create and discreate identities in your Shell
to change your BEing and therefore your Causal Sequences = Life.**

You had to block and counter-create your Essence to reduce your BEing, your WPVLJ, down to that of a human being so you can explore the negative side of the Creation. When BEing Essence, your original and True BEing, you cannot experience anything negative. You cannot have Games, problems, conflicts, Drama and UPS. You reduce your divine Essence down to human by creating a cloud of energy, a Shell of ECRED around you-consciousness. That Shell acts upon you to produce all your experience of being human. Your Shell is like a computer program that paints on the screen of your consciousness-experience all your human experience and behaviors.

In your Shell is programmed everything that makes you not only a human being, but a *unique* human being. Since the beginning of history, there have been about 110,000,000,0000 human beings on the planet, and each one is a unique combination of characteristics. In your Shell are programmed: your personality, your character, your likes and dislikes, your talents and ineptitudes, all your negative identities, all your negative emotions, your traumas, your habits, your desires, your values, your addictions and compulsions, your memories, etc. – EVERYTHING you are and experience as a human being.

Illustration: The Shell of realities that generate for the psycan
his human identity and experience.

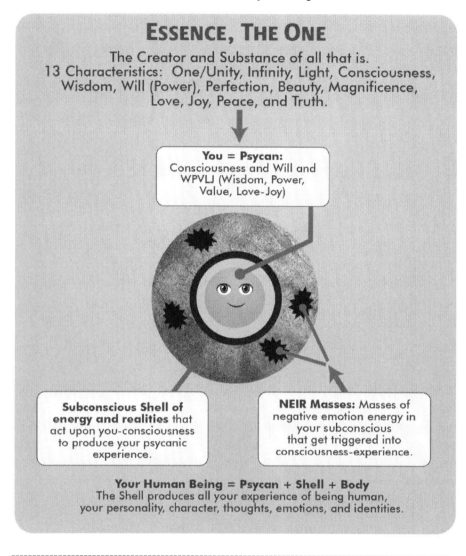

ESSENCE, THE ONE

The Creator and Substance of all that is.
13 Characteristics: One/Unity, Infinity, Light, Consciousness,
Wisdom, Will (Power), Perfection, Beauty, Magnificence,
Love, Joy, Peace, and Truth.

You = Psycan:
Consciousness and Will and
WPVLJ (Wisdom, Power,
Value, Love-Joy)

**Subconscious Shell of
energy and realities** that
act upon you-consciousness
to produce your psycanic
experience.

NEIR Masses: Masses of
negative emotion energy in
your subconscious
that get triggered into
consciousness-experience.

Your Human Being = Psycan + Shell + Body
The Shell produces all your experience of being human,
your personality, character, thoughts, emotions, and identities.

You are the creator of your Shell, your HIC. Most of it you created before you incarnated, when you planned this lifetime. You stocked your HIC with the characteristics, talents and affinities, you need for this lifetime. Other parts of the Shell you develop as you grow up, for example childhood traumas, as well as education and trainings.

The main factor in your achieving No-Power, ergo able to maintain Game Conditions (no results) and Dramas, is your NEIRs, your counter-creations to Essence WPVLJ. Your Shell is set up to generate Drama; to restore Power, you re-create your NEIRs in your Shell. Your innate Divine Essence of Being is

Power; you have to counter-create Who You Really Are in order to BE human. **This is why discreation is more important the creation by eliminating all the negative from your life and restoring you to Power. YOU MUST ELIMINATE NEGATIVES before worrying about positives. Trying to create positives to plaster over negatives does not work.**

Using BTT, you-psycan go into your Shell to discreate the negatives and then create positives in their place. You can change anything in your Shell and so transform your **human being-experience-life**. This is what we are teaching you to do in Psycanics; and if you choose to advance that far, even more so in Essentiality.

Your Negative Essence Identity Reality (NEIR) Masses

As we mentioned before, your "human being", your HIC, is not alive! It is a great structure of identities, a great Shell of ECRE, that encase you-psycan and generate your human experience. You can go into this Shell and create and discreate its ECRE at will; this is what we are teaching you how to do. What you will most want to discreate are your NEIRs, your Negative Essence Identity Realities. These counter-create your divine Essence, your innate Power so you can be a (relatively) powerless human being.

You are a spirit with the fundamental and universal spiritual characteristics of Wisdom (includes intelligence), Will-Power, Self-Value, and Love-Joy. These are abbreviated WPVLJ). We call the spiritual entity that you are a **psycan**. As a "child of God", you-psycan are a powerful creator of all your experience and of your life. You create your life through the Causal Sequence, starting with your BEing.

And that, Who You Really Are, was your Great Challenge in BEcoming a human being! You cannot BE Who You Really Are, a psycan with his Essential Nature of WPVLJ and BE a human being. NO! You have to counter-create your Essence to lower your WPVLJ down to that of a human being, which is not just low on the Polarity Scale of BEing, but is negative. You do this with NEIRs:

What most counter-creates your Essence is your NEIRs.
What you are most going to be discreating with BTT are
your NEIRS.

By BEing your NEIRs, you create the illusion of being a human being: ignorant, powerless, negative value (unworthy) and UPS instead of Love-Joy.

Your NEIRS are four (4) great masses of negative identities; identities which counter-create, deny, or suppress your true, spiritual, innate nature of Wisdom, Power, Value, Love-Joy (WPVLJ). Your objective is to discreate these and so restore to BEing to positive WPVLJ. Your positive BEing of WPVLJ will naturally manifest positive Causal Sequences in all areas of your life.

These four identity masses reside in your subconscious, outside of your normal range of perception. However, negative events can trigger, activate, them into your consciousness-experience, where you experience them as charges of negative emotions. However, **the negative identity (NEIR) is always present within the neg-emo.**

We call these neg identity masses:
NEIRs: Negative Essence Identity Realities.

Your NEIRs are the source of all your problems,
conflicts, and UPS in life.

Identities

Your BEing consists of all your identities. **Your BEing is the sum total of all your identities.** Your identities are your declarations, creations, of what you are and what you are not. This will become clearer in the next chapters with their examples of BEing and identities.

Your identities are your causal element in your many Causal Sequences and therefore in all your Arenas, in all your life. *Although they are not quite the same, we can use "BEing" and "identities" as synonyms.*

Here is the secret to immense power over your experience and life:

Remember that life operates: BE→FEEL→THINK→REL-DO→HAVE:

➢ [Positive identities= positive states of Being] naturally produce positive results in all the other Arenas of Life. Positive identities produce positive emotions that energize wise THINKing that guides action (DO) to produce the desired results (HAVE).

➢ [Negative identities= negative states of BEing] naturally produce negative results in all the other Arenas. Neg BEing produces negative emotions (UPS) that distort THINKing and wisdom, and lead to negative actions (neg DOing) which naturally produce poor results (neg HAVE).

CHANGE YOUR IDENTITY (BEing) in any Causal Sequence and all the rest of that Causal Sequence changes automatically. (Change your NEIRs with which you are operating your relationships now, and your relationships will change.)

CHANGE YOUR IDENTITIES (BEing) and
YOUR LIFE WILL CHANGE.

TRANSFORM YOUR BEING AND
YOUR LIFE WILL TRANSFORM.

WORKS LIKE MAGIC!

Any sufficiently advanced technology is indistinguishable from magic.

Why are your NEIRs so powerful, so important? They counter-act your divine nature of Essence=WPVLJ so that you-psycan can create and explore the negative side of the Creation (anti-Essence, anti-power, Game Conditions, Drama, UPS, relations problems, anti-love, failure, evil, etc.). BTT (Being Transformation Technology) is a precision system of how to change your BEing by discreating your NEIRs (your anti-Essence) and re-creating your Self in PEIRs = restore your Essence.

Psycanics

You are studying psycanics. Psycanics is the **physics of human trans-physical ECRE.** Your trans-physical ECRE include your identities, self-image, self-esteem, everything in your subconscious, your emotions, intelligence, memories, thoughts, creativity, relationships, love, and happiness - to name a few.

With BTT, you learn to take *any* negative experience in *any* Arena and track it back to the causal NEIR of that undesired experience. You can then discreate that NEIR and then re-create yourself to BE a **Positive Essence Identity Reality (PEIR)**. PEIRs are identities that confirm your WPVLJ. All your other Arenas (emotions, thoughts, actions, and results) will then naturally transform to conform to your new, positive BEing, to your PEIR.

It's MAGIC!

YOU CAN PROVE ALL THIS TO YOURSELF BEYOND ALL DOUBT USING YOUR OWN LIFE AS YOUR LABORATORY.

Backtracking any negative experience or behavior in any Arena to your negative causal identity (NEIR), then discreating that state of BEing and re-creating yourself in a PEIR is relatively simple, very fast, and highly effective compared to any other form of psycho-therapy.

Realities Cause Experience.
Experience is the Effect of Realities on Consciousness.

Identities are one form of realities;
they are your ECRE about your Self.

You can create and discreate your identities, therefore your BEing.

Transform your BEing and your Causal Sequences auto-transform.

Note: Do not confuse reality with truth: they are two very different things! Realities you can create and discreate at will; truth is immovable. *(We will have a chapter on truth versus reality later because the confusion is one of the 7 Conditions that will stop discreation.)*

Let's repeat some of the above because they are center points of the entire book:

Life operates according to the Causal Sequence of
BE→FEEL→THINK→RELATE / DO→HAVE.

What you are learning to do is to find the root cause behind any negative experience or behavior in your life, in any Arena. That root cause will always be a negative state of your BEing, a negative identity, a NEIR, of which there are only four flavors.

Once located your NEIR *in your experience (not in mind!)*, you can discreate it; cause it to cease to exist.

You will then re-create your Self in a positive identity, one that affirms your WPVLJ (called PEIRs: Positive Essence Identity Reality).

That Causal Sequence will automatically change itself from negative experiences to all positive.

Repeat this on every activations of your negative emotions, and you will eventually eliminate all NEIRs and have re-created your Self in all PEIRs.

— —

Let's summarize what you are learning to do:

1- To TRACE BACK any NEGATIVE EXPERIENCE or BEHAVIOR in your life to your CAUSAL NEIR.

2- DISCREATE your NEIR which _permanently_ eliminates that quantity of negative ECRE from your BEing.

3- RE-CREATE your SELF in the appropriate PEIR.

4- WATCH that CAUSAL SEQUENCE TRANSFORM TO POSITIVE IN ALL THE OTHER ARENAS.

5- REPEAT until you no longer have any NEIRS, about 400 hours of BTT (usually done an hour a day in less than 2 years).

———————————————————————————————

Note: For any particular situation (one Causal Sequence) the discreation of the neg ID can take anywhere from 40 minutes to various hours (depending on various factors). To eliminate ALL neg identities in ALL your Causal Sequences, which completely transforms your life, takes about 100 hours per identity mass. You have four neg identity masses: Wisdom, Power, Value, and Love-Joy: 4 x 100 hours = about 400 hours of BTT. Students of the PLTS (Psycanics Life Transformation System) usually achieve these 400 hours in 2 years or less in the School depending on how much time they dedicate weekly to their discreation and re-creation.

BTT is the Fulcrum and Lever Capable of Transforming your World

Archimedes, the Greek mathematician and physicist, is reputed to have said that given a fulcrum and a long-enough lever, he could move the earth. Your BEing is lever for your life that controls your life. BTT is the lever that more than moves your BEing; it allows you to transform it to all positive.

12- Examples of BEing

The purpose of this chapter is to clarify BEing by giving you some examples.

1- Are you BEing intelligent and wise, or BEing foolish and stupid? If you can't feel which you are being, look at your life, at your decisions, results, and circumstances. Do they reflect wisdom or foolishness?

2- Are you BEing someone who loves learning, or BEing someone who resists it? Are you BEing someone who is good at learning, or someone who is BEing poor at it?

3- Are you BEing a fast learner? - or someone who finds learning difficult, i.e. BEing someone who can't learn easily?

4- Are you BEing the creator of your life - or are you BEing the victim of life (assigning agency to others and events)?

5- Are you BEing responsible for the quality of your relationships, or are you blaming the other for causing the problems (victim again)?

6- Are you BEing always serene, or are you BEing reactive, irritable, angry?

7- Are you BEing good enough, or not good enough?

8- Are you BEing equal to all others; or BEing less than, or better than others? (Both more than and less than are negative states of BEing) (How do you feel about yourself — equal or less than-- in different situations: examples: around rich people, in fancy places, with someone of the opposite sex you are attracted to, in business, in sports, etc.?

9- Are you BEing capable and powerful; or BEing incapable, weak or a failure?

10- Are you BEing a success; or are you BEing mediocre; or BEing a failure? (Examples of people exploring failure include people in prison, drug addicts, and homeless. Failure is a valid experience. All experiences are valid and contribute to the infinite variety of experiences that is the Creation. No state of BEing or experience is Bad-Should Not Be (abbreviated Bad-SNB). All experiences are deliberate, if unconscious, creations of the psycan. There are no coincidences or accidents. Everything that exists is a creation. See Essentiality I.)

11- Are you BEing excellent in all that you are and do; or are you BEing mediocre - or worse?

12- Are you BEing valuable, worthy and deserving; or do you feel you are less valuable than others, unworthy, or undeserving? If you feel those, you are BEing them; they are NEIRs.

13- Are you BEing humble; or are you living in the negative ego of believing yourself as BEing more or better than others? (Negative ego is fatal to love, relationships, and happiness, but that is a story for Essentiality.)

14- Are you BEing loving, or are you BEing spiteful or hateful?

15- Are you BEing an integrator and unifier of people, or a divider and separator? Are you BEing love or are you BEing a bigot, one who invalidates, rejects, even hates others for superficial skin, race or gender differences?

16- Are you always BEing honest, or are you BEing a liar, cheat, or thief? (There are always consequences in your own happiness for giving any form of negative energy to others.)

17- Are you BEing love and therefore DOing good; or are you BEing evil by emanating negative energy or doing things that harm others or the world?

18- Are you BE-FEELing yourself a good person; or do you, at least sometimes, BE-FEEL that you are a bad person? (or bad parent, or bad son/daughter, or bad whatever your profession is).

Most people do not recognize the importance of BEing. However, your BEing dictates the rest of your life, your FEEL, THINK, RELATE, DO, HAVE. Here is why:

You-the BEing (psycan) are the ONLY Causal element in your life; you are the CREATOR of your life. (We will cover this thoroughly in Book 2). A Law of Creation is:

You cannot create or manifest anything that would conflict with, contradict, WHO YOU ARE BEING.

For example: if you have identities such as: I am unable to earn enough; I am less than others; I am unworthy; I am not smart enough, money is scarce; you have to work hard to earn money; only the corrupt are rich; etc.; you will have trouble manifesting money because having lots of money easily contradicts who you are BEing.

Just growing up in a poor family is enough to infect you with negative identities and realities about money; they will be absorbed from others and implanted in your subconscious.

As a psycan, you are only Essence. Everything else you are BEing is a creation, down from human being itself, through your character and personality, down to your identities and all your psycanic realities.

Control your BEing and your control your life: it's magic.

To control your BEing, discreate your negative identities and create positive ones.

Fortunately, you don't need to control all the above states of BEing. You need to control just FOUR (4) states of BEing: your four Essence identity polarities: PEIRs <> NEIRs. The four identities are:

1- **Wisdom** (includes intelligence, knowledge, and ability to learn).

2- **Power** (the ability to produce any desired result in your life).

3- **Value**: your experience of yourself as being valuable, worthy, deserving, rather than the opposites, or less than others.

4- **Love**, which is the Good<>Bad person polarity. Being **good** is being lovable, the opposite of which is being a bad person or role (parent, son, daughter, or in your profession). Bad people are not lovable, do not deserve the respect or others or the good things of life. As person who has his "I am Bad" identity activated will live in self-sabotage and creating negatives in his life to punish himself.

Now that we have seen BEing, we need to go to what comprises your BEing, particularly your Essence identities, your PEIRs<>NEIRs. To understand them, we must first understand Polarity, our next chapter.

13- Polarity

It is impossible to understand existence, to control your life, to discreate, or to cease to suffer, without understanding Polarity. The Creation is full of polarities. You, yourself, are a polar being with a positive, light and love side; and a negative, dark, anti-love side. Your BEing is polar; your PEIRs<>NEIRs are a Polarity. To be able to discreate your negative identities and so end your negative BE FEEL THINK REL-DO and HAVE, you must understand and apply the Laws of Polarity.

Definition: Polarity

A polarity is any experience stretched in two opposing directions, towards two extremes or poles, usually denominated positive and negative. **This "stretching" creates a scale, a spectrum, of gradients of that experience between those two poles.** Thus, out of one thing, an entire range of positive and of negative variations of that experience is created, greatly enriching the Creation and its variety of experiences. (Infinite variety of realities→experiences, ever changing, remember, is the Purpose of the Creation.)

Polarity is pure genius: the Creator at work.

There are four ways to indicate polarity in psycanics. They are:

> #1- "<>" between the names of the two poles: "light<>dark".
>
> #2- "+/-" after the phenomenon: "emotions +/- "
> meaning the positive and the negative emotions.
>
> #3- The prefix "**neg**-": neg-energy, neg-love, neg-power,
> neg-emotion (also abbreviated neg-emo).
>
> #4- The prefix "**anti-**": anti-love, anti-power, anti-wisdom, etc.
>
> Thus, the opposite of love can be expressed as "neg-love" or "anti-love".
> (The opposite of love is also called "evil".)

An Example of a FU Polarity: Temperature

The temperature spectrum is a good example of a physical universe polarity. We stretch "temperature" out in two directions, towards the two poles of hot and cold. This creates a range, a spectrum, of possibilities of different temperatures, from absolute zero at minus 459 F, to over 10,000,000 degrees F in the center of the hottest stars.

Illustration: The Temperature Polarity Spectrum

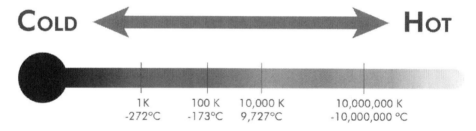

More examples of physical experience polarities and spectrums are:
- hard<>soft
- light<>dark
- rich<>poor
- healthy<>sick
- young<>old
- loud<>quiet
- the color spectrum
- the EMR (electro-magnetic radiation) spectrum

Two Examples of Psycanic Polarities: Love and Emotions.

Love is a polarity; it has a positive and a negative side.

The positive side is positive love (+love or just "love") which includes all forms of positive energy and actions that increase the well-being of others and the world. +Love starts with giving space to others to be as they are and not-be as they are not. It then ascends a scale of more and more positive energy output as shown in its illustration overleaf.

The negative polarity of love is neg-love, anti-love, or evil. Neg-love is all forms of negative energy and action, from mild dislike to bullets and bombs. It is everything that harms, damages, destroys, causes suffering, or otherwise decreases the aliveness, the well-being of others or the world. For example, damaging the environment for personal or corporate profit is neg-love, is evil.

Note: Neg-love/evil is not "Bad-Wrong-Should Not BE"! (abbreviated Bad-SNB). It is a valid and rich experience within the infinity of creations in the universe, and it is essential so that pos-love can exist. There is no good and love, without evil, one of the laws of polarity we will soon come to.

Emotions

Your emotions are a polarity. You do not have many emotions! **All emotions are the same energy stretched over its polarity spectrum**, just as all temperature as the measure of the internal velocity of atoms in the object. All emotions are variations of one thing, of the one emotion energy.

What are your emotions?

Your emotions are self-love. **Your emotions+/- are the polarity of self-love energy+/-,** stretched out between the positive pole of ecstasy and negative of deepest hate.

> Note: your feelings for others are NOT love for them; they are your love for your Self triggered by who you are BEing in relation to them. Your love for others is how you treat them, not how you feel about them. We will see this in more depth later.

On the positive side are all the positive emotions such as we have energies like contentment, satisfaction, interest, enthusiasm, passion, and joy. These are happiness.

On the negative side, we have the **five families** of negative emotions: anger, fear, sorrow, guilt, and depression, with many variations within each family. See the illustration.

Illustration: The Self-Love Polarity and the Emotions Polarity are one and the same energy.

THE LOVE POLARITY

POSITIVE LOVE

All forms of positive energy and actions that create, build, care for, or grow others and contribute to the world.

Includes: listen, teach, help, support, giving service.

All the positive emotions are positive self-love energies.

NEGATIVE LOVE OR ANTI-LOVE

All forms of negative energy and actions that harm, damage, cause suffering, or destroy.

Includes: anger, hate, bigotry, lying, stealing, cheating, corruption, tyranny, war, etc. Aka Evil.

All the negative emotions are anti-love for self.

The Emotions Polarity, the Self-Love Energy Polarity and
the Happiness⬦UPS Polarity are all the same thing,
the same energy, the same experience. Love is the ONLY happiness
there is, and all Love must start with Self-Love.
You cannot give to others what you do not have.

THE EMOTIONS POLARITY

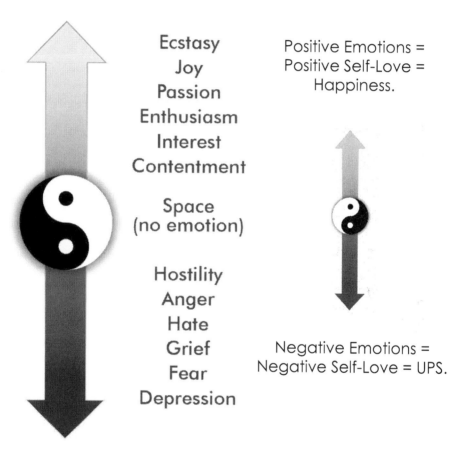

Ecstasy
Joy
Passion
Enthusiasm
Interest
Contentment

Space
(no emotion)

Hostility
Anger
Hate
Grief
Fear
Depression

Positive Emotions =
Positive Self-Love =
Happiness.

Negative Emotions =
Negative Self-Love = UPS.

Your emotions are the only happiness or suffering
that exist for you.
You are the creator of your emotions, positive and negative.
What you have created, you can discreate.
You discreate negative emotions by discreating their causal
state of BEing. (BE→FEEL).

More examples of psycanic experience polarities are:

> Positive<>Negative,
> Love<>Evil,
> Pleasure<>Pain,
> Wisdom<>Stupidity,
> Power<>No-Power (Incompetence)
> Happiness<>Sufferings,
> Success<>Failure,
> Friends<>Enemies,
> and a very important one for couple relationships: **Yin<>Yang**.

Definitions:

Positive: that which is pleasant, desired, creative, constructive, productive. All that is **ectropic**; all that increases the organization and energy state of a system (which requires intelligent Cause; energy and matter by themselves are entropic).

Negative: that which is unpleasant, painful, undesired, counter-productive, harmful, or destructive. All that is willfully **entropic**: decreases usable energy and increases disorder and chaos, or homogeneity. **Negative is NOT Bad-SNB!** By the Laws of Polarity, negatives must exist for positives to exist, and they are valid experiences in themselves. Entropy is also a necessary element of the Creation and is not Bad-SNB itself; only when caused by humans to the detriment of the Good.

Bad: that which **Should Not Be (SNB)**, should not exist, *apparently* justifying the use of resistance and negative energy to stop, change, punish or destroy that "bad" entity. (We say *apparently* because under the Laws of Love, negative energy, negative love, is **never** justified.)

Bad-SNB: abbreviation for "Bad, Wrong, and therefore Should-Not-Be". This is always a creation, an opinion, a hallucination of the human mind. In the Truth of the Creation, nothing is ever Bad-SNB, including evil itself. There can never BE something that Should Not BE.

> Whenever you label something Bad-SNB, you are saying that thing should not exist. If it exists, it has the approval of Essence (God) to exist: if Her Omnipotence did not want something to exist, it would not. In religious terms, that is the sin of arrogance, egotism, pride, hubris. Ask yourself: "Who am I to tell God what should be and should not be in Her Creation?" "Who am I to deny Essence that form of experience?" *(We will come back to all this in the chapter on Bad-SNB.)*

Love: There are two areas of love: love for Self, and love for others and the world. Your love for others is your **actions (DO)**: how you treat them and the energies you use with them. **Love for others and the world includes all forms of positive energy that unite, care for, help, better, and grow the world around you.**

Your love for yourself is your emotions +/-. (For example, anger is anti-love for your Self that may motivate you to act negatively (give anti-love) to others. We will explain this in great depth in a later chapter.

Advanced concept: Evil: The best word for the polar opposite of Love, aka neg-love, anti-love, is "evil". Evil is all forms of negative energy and actions that are entropic; that harm, damage, cause suffering, or destroy the Greater Good. Evil includes anger, hate, bigotry, division and marginalization, inequality, injustice, criminality (theft, fraud, etc.) political and corporate greed and corruption, killing, war, tyranny, slavery, genocide, etc. **Look at the planet and you will see evil is a very common and popular human activity.**

Two of the Laws of Polarity

#1- The Law of Mutual Creation and Indispensability:

Each side of a polarity creates the other.

BOTH SIDES OF A POLARITY MUST EXIST
for either side to exist, for the polarity to exist.

It is IMPOSSIBLE TO HAVE ONE SIDE
OF A POLARITY WITHOUT THE OTHER.

It is IMPOSSIBLE for positives to exist without negatives.

Ergo: The negative polarities are not Bad-SNB! Negatives are necessary, essential, to the Creation, ergo they are GOOD! Without them, the Creation would be greatly diminished because there would be no polarities, neither positives nor negatives of any kind.

Furthermore, **negatives are rich and valid experiences in themselves.** You-human go to movies and sports for the Drama and to experience losing. You-psycan incarnated on Earth to explore negatives: Neg-WPVLJ, to lose some of your Games, and to savor DUPS. The truth is that we-psycans love DUPS, so much so that most psycans are unwilling to change from DUPS in their human lives to Power→Results→Satisfaction. For example, psycanics is very unpopular with Victims (TT): it destroys the Drama.

#2- As both sides of a polarity _must_ exist, we have Law #2:

To resist one side of a polarity
(for 3 examples: your NEIRs, your neg-emo = UPS, or evil)
is to resist life as it is and as it must be.

Your only UPS in life is your own resistance
to what is, above all, to your NEIRs.

All your neg-emotions= UPS are
your resistances to your own NEIRs.

Law of Neg-Energy:
Resistance causes pain and persistence.

Does resisting life as it is and must be, i.e. resisting the negatives, and thereby creating one's own UPS, qualify as anti-wisdom in your opinion?

NIsGOB CharPriCon

NIsGOB CharPriCon is the acronym for **Nothing Is Good or Bad and everything has Characteristics, Prices and Consequences.**

For example, violating the Laws of Polarity is not Bad-SNB and has its prices and consequences. These include the Hallucinating Bad-SNB, the creation of resistance, pain, suffering; loss of power to discrete, and persistence of negative realities you would like to discreate. We will come back to all of these in more detail later and their respective chapters.

The Most Important Polarity: The Essence Polarity of Being (EPB)

The most important polarity in all of the Creation is the Essence Polarity of Being (EPB) comprising the 13 Primordial Characteristics of Essence (Oneness/Unity, Infinity, Light, Consciousness, Wisdom, Will (Power), Perfection, Beauty, Magnificence, Love, Joy, Peace, and Truth. The full concept of the EPB (Essence Polarity of BEing) is advanced spiritual knowledge beyond the scope of this book; here we need only concern ourselves with the four Characteristics that determine and dominate your human experience: WPVLJ: Wisdom, Power, Value, and Love-Joy. (We are combining Love and Joy because they are almost indistinguishable.)

The Essence Polarity of Being (EPB) is so important because it is your level of experience and expression of your Essence, your Divinity; here of the four Primordial Characteristics: Wisdom, Power, Value, and Love-Joy.

**The negative polarity of these four identities (WPVLJ)
are your NEIRS and
dominate your negative Causal Sequences,
ergo your human experience and behaviors.**

Relationships

The discreation of your NEIRs and your re-creation of Self in PEIRs transforms your BEing. Transform your BEing and your life (which consists of Causal Sequences) transforms automatically to conform to your new BEing.

The source of the great majority of problems and conflicts in your relationships is your External Quest to try to control your BE-FEEL by dictating to others how they should BFTRDH as part of your Existential Imperative efforts to Not-BE NEIRs and trying to BE PEIRs.

To see this:

- How many people in your life are trying to control you, to dictate to you how you should BFTRDH?

- How much do they do so with anti-love (neg-energy): invalidation, anger, demands, guilting, criticism, ostracization, punishment, etc.?

- How do you respond? cooperating and obeying, or resisting with neg-energy or your own?

- Do all these demands, control, and anti-love improve or deteriorate your relationships?

- In the same way, they are doing all that to you; you are doing all that to them, whether you recognize it or not.

- We will see all this in detail in Book 3.

Your NEIRs are the subject of our next chapter

14- PEIRs <> NEIRs

The Essence Identities Polarities

We restate your objectives to BE magically powerful over your life:

1.   Learn to TRACE BACK any NEGATIVE EXPERIENCE or BEHAVIOR in your life to your CAUSAL NEIR.

2.   DISCREATE that NEIR which _permanently_ eliminates it from your BEing, as well as its associated neg-emo = UPS.

3.   RE-CREATE your Self (your BEing) in the appropriate PEIR, which will automatically produce positive self-love = positive emotion = happiness.

4.   ENERGIZE your desired experiences in the other Arenas of that Causal Sequence. These will manifest easily.

In this chapter, we are studying the nature of your negative BE in your Causal Sequences. Your negative BEing consists of **four negative identity masses,** your **NEIR** masses. These are the root cause of your problems and DUPS in life.

The Four Spiritual Characteristics of WPVLJ

You are an ego-ized individualization[2] of the One Infinite Consciousness, of the Creator and Essence of all that is. She has 13 Primordial Characteristics: Truth, Oneness/Unity, Infinity, Light, Consciousness, Wisdom, Will/Power, Beauty, Magnificence, Love, Peace, Joy, and Truth. Note how when people report their mystical experiences, they report one or more of these Characteristics. (The Pew Institute reports that almost 50% of the population has had a mystical experience at least once. Graduates of the Essentiality School of Accelerated Enlightenment have them frequently; they can feel Essence at will.)

Of the 13 Characteristics, 4 of them dominate your human existence. These are:

Wisdom: the ability to foresee consequences and choose then appropriate action to achieve your desired outcome. Wisdom includes intelligence, knowledge (and therefore study and learning), intuition, creativity and problem-solving.

Power: your ability to produce your desired result in any area of life (relationships, money, success, health, etc.) It includes your power to create and discreate your realities which is what we are seeking in this book.

Value: your sense of self-worth, of dignity and worthiness. It is your sense of self-esteem with identity polarities such as: I am important<>unimportant; I am worthy<>I am unworthy; I am deserving<>I am undeserving; I am equal<>I am less than others. (Value is part of Magnificence.)

Love-Joy, which is also Goodness<>Badness as a person LJ is your internal experience, conscious or subconscious, sense of Being GOOD and therefore love-able, starting with love-able by your Self; or your experience of BEing the opposite, of being BAD (or evil) and therefore unlove-able, starting with to yourself. Essence is Love and as Love is the ONLY happiness that exists; She is Joy. Your emotions are your self-love+/-; your positive emotions are happiness; your negative emotions are your only UPS in life. BEing BAD destroy your love for Self and therefore your happiness.

All Four Characteristics Are Polarities
and All the Laws of Polarity Apply.

---

[2] Ego individualization: The nature of ego and individuality and how you-psycan are a spark or particle of the One Infinite Essence BEing is described in Essentiality.

Your Essence identities+/-, NEIRs and PEIRs, are realities, are ECRE, and are polarities. All the laws of PECRED apply, as well as all the Laws of Polarity.

Reminder of definition of Reality, necessary to understand identities:

Reality: Everything that exists, psycanic and physical, is a reality. A reality is any mass of energy modulated to create its flavor of experience. All thoughts and emotions are realities.

All realities are creations: somebody, somewhere, sometime, created it. You are the creator of ALL your psycanic realities. Anything you have created, you can discreate. Realities must not be confused with truth; they are rarely truth. Your NEIRs will sometimes feel like truth; they are not; never believe in them.

An identity is a special case of a reality, your reality about your Self.
All the laws of PECRED (creation and discreation) apply.

Identity: any ECRE (*energy → creation → reality → experience*) you have about who you are, or are not. You are the creator of all your identity-realities. You will recognize your identities because you feel (experience) them. Always keep in mind: Discreation occurs only in experience, never in mind. (The BTT Course trains you to perceive the difference and how to stay out of mind.)

Negative Essence Identities: Your Negative Essence Ids are your ECRE of who you are that negate your BEing Essence in any of the 13 Essence Characteristics of BEing. However, we are only interested in the 4 Characteristics that most affect human existence: WPVLJ. In Essence, all the Characteristics are Absolute: there is no polarity. However, in the Creation, the Characteristics, the identities, are polarities. Thus, we have PEIRs ◇ NEIRs:

• PEIR: Positive Essence Identity Reality. These are your identities (creations of self, of BEing) that affirm your divine Essence of Wisdom, Power, Value, Love-Joy (WPVLJ).

• NEIR: Negative Essence Identity Reality. These are your identities, your ECRE, that counter-create, suppress or deny your innate, original, divine nature of WPVLJ.

This will become clearer studying the following table of PEIRs ◇ NEIRs.

Realities cause experience.
Experience is the effect of realities on consciousness is to say:

Identities cause your experience of Self.
They comprise your BEing,
all that you are BEing and Not-Being.

They are the most powerful of all your creations:
they initiate all your Causal Sequences and manifest

your results in the other Arenas –

even though most people are at best only vaguely conscious of them!

To change Who You Are, your experience of Self, your self-image and self-esteem, discreate your neg identities (NEIRs) and re-create your Self in positive ones (PEIRs).

Resisting your NEIRS – which is what all UHBs do -- DOES NOT WORK. It energizes and persists them.

You are the creator and the discreator of your ECRE including your identities. Discreation occurs only in experience (consciousness), never in mind.

Two important understandings

#1 - Not thoughts or beliefs! Your NEIRs are not thoughts or beliefs which are very light, low-mass realities. Thoughts come and go quickly. **Your NEIRs are large masses of energy-reality,** usually dormant in your subconscious.

Your NEIR masses activate into, jump into, your consciousness-experience when there is a trigger event in your life. Even though you never feel more than a small fraction of your NEIR masses at a time, even those fractions are more powerful than any thought. A thought or belief you can change at will; you will need about 400 hours of BTT to eliminate all your NEIR. On discreating them, you will be free of all the negative human emotions.

> We have here one of the shortcomings of various psychologies and therapy techniques. They do detect identities, but treat them as thoughts and beliefs, which are supposedly easy to change or to over-create, for example, with affirmations. Were it so easy!

#2- The expression linguistic of the NEIR is not the NEIR. The NEIR is an experience, not a thought or a mental image, much less the words used to label it. The linguistic expression, the verbal description, can vary from person to person. **Your NEIRs are realities, masses of energy**, in your subconscious that producing your _experience_ of BEing that way. In the same way that the word "dog" is not the animal; words, sentences, labels, *and thoughts* are not the NEIR.

There are many ways to express, to label, the experience of a NEIR, as shown by the examples in the table below. There are many ways not listed and very occasionally an explorer will come up with a new one we pilots have not heard before. Just keep in mind that the **NEIR is not the words; it is the experience of a reality mass, of BEing that way.**

The Four Anti-WPVLJ states of BEing:

1.   Anti-Wisdom: It is the experience of not being intelligent or not being wise, or being mentally slow or stupid or not being able to learn.

2.   Anti-Power: It is the experience of not being able, of being unable, being impotent, or being weak or being a failure.

3.   Anti-Value: It is the experience of being of less value, less worth, less deserving, less important than others, or of not being paid much attention.

4.   Anti-Love: It is the experience of being a _bad_ person, or _bad_ role (parent, son, daughter, spouse, carpenter, business person, whatever).

Table of examples of expressions of the four Essence identity polarities = PEIRs <> NEIRs. The NEIR is not the expression; it is ECRE.

TABLE OF EXAMPLES OF EXPRESSIONS OF THE FOUR ESSENCE IDENTITY POLARITIES = PEIRs <> NEIRs

	Wisdom Intelligence	Power	Value	Love (Good<>Bad)
PEIRs	I am smart / intelligent. I learn easily and quickly. I am wise. I am knowledgeable. I understand things quickly.	I am powerful. I can (whatever). I am able. I am capable. I am strong. I am a success.	I am valuable. I am worthy. I am deserving. I am good enough.	I am lovable. I am a good person and therefore lovable.
NEIRs	I am not smart / intelligent enough. I am less intelligent than others. I am stupid. I am ignorant. I don't understand well. Study is hard.	I am not powerful. I can't (whatever). I am unable. I am incapable. I am weak. I am a failure.	I am less than others. I am unworthy. I am underserving. I am not good enough.	I am bad. I am a bad person and therefore unlovable. (Bad in role: spouse, son, daughter, lawyer, etc.)

Remember: The linguistic expression (words, sentences) are not important. Identities are masses of energy (realities) that produce **EXPERIENCE**. It is the experience. Different people express their identity experiences in different words.

Your negative energies (NEIRs and emotions) **are not Bad-SNB**! On the contrary, they are good and are necessary experiences for three reasons:

1- They are valid creations and rich experiences in themselves. You-psycan came to Earth to explore negative experiences., e.g. No-Power and Drama. You cannot know such experiences when you are in your Essence.

2- The negative sides of all polarities must exist for the positive side to exist. Remember, it is impossible to have one side of a polarity without the other. The Creation would not only be greatly diminished, impoverished, without both sides, but it could not even exist as we know it; there would be no positives either.

3- As a psycan, you must alternate between the two sides to refresh and renew your experience of the positive. You are doing this by coming to Earth to explore the negatives so that you can return to Love and experience Her fully again. (Alternation of Polarities is explained in the Essentiality books.)

Purpose of your NEIRs

The purpose of your NEIRs is to reduce your BEing from your original, divine nature, down to that of a human being. The purpose of being a human is so that you can that you can play the Human Game, live the Human Movie, and explore DUPS (Drama and UPS). Remember, you-spirit (psycan) come to Earth for Drama.

To BEcome a human being, you-psycan had to **counter-create** your WPVLJ to lower your Wisdom, Power, Value and Love-Joy to human levels (which are very low and even negative). Your NEIRs suppress your original nature of WPVLJ; they "lower" you from divine to human.

Your discreation of your NEIRS as your counter-creations to divine Essence of WPVL is the second most powerful thing you can do in life. (The most powerful is to experience Essence, but this is the province of Essentiality.) As your identities comprise your BEing, discreating your NEIRs transform your BEing in your Causal Sequences. Transform your BEing and you will transform your life. The BTT course trains you, step-by-step, in how to do all of this.

An SEB (Spiritually Enlightened Being) is one who has learned and applied all the things in this book and the more advanced ones in the Essentiality School of Accelerated Enlightenment. She has awakened from the illusion that she is only a human being and recovered her experience of herself as a psycan and creator. She has discreated all her negative identities and therefore all her negative emotions. She has re-created herself in the "image and likeness" of God by restoring her WPVLJ, her original nature of Essence.

15- FEEL-ing: Your Emotions

The arena of FEEL in the Causal Sequence of Life comprises all your emotions, positive and negative. In this chapter we will explain what your emotions are, what causes them, and how to eliminate your negative ones forever.

Your emotions are all one phenomenon, one energy. You do not have many different kinds of emotional energy; all emotions are the same energy stretched in the directions of positive and of negative to create a polarity spectrum of many flavors of the one emotional energy. **All the Laws of PECRED and of Polarity apply.**

Your emotions are like the visible light spectrum where a prism breaks one white light up into all the colors.

Illustration: The One Emotion Energy polarized into a spectrum.

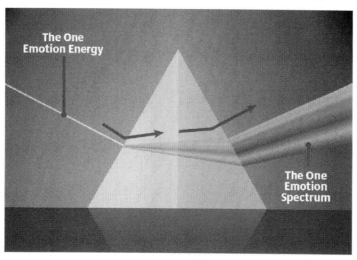

The positive emotions are degrees and flavors of happiness and include contentment, satisfaction, amusement, interest, enjoyment, excitement, pride, enthusiasm, passion, and joy.

The negative emotions are UPS. They are the only UPS you know. They include hostility, anger, rage, hate, anxiety, fear, worry, guilt, regret, shame, remorse, sadness, loneliness, sorrow, grief, depression, and apathy, among others. ("Negative emotion" will sometimes be abbreviated "neg-emo".)

Definition: **Activation, MOD** (Moment of Dolor (Latin for Pain): A MOD or activation is the sudden movement within your Space of BEing of a NEIR mass. The mass jumps from your {subconscious=out-of-perception} to your {consciousness = perception-experience}. You experience a NEIR mass primarily as neg-emo, but the NEIR (or NEIRs) is always there.

Definition: **Trigger event, trigger:** The trigger event is anything that occurs in your external or internal experience (it can a thought). You-psycan, unconsciously, adopt a state of BEing, an identity, a NEIR, to relation to the event. That NEIR is accompanied by a charge of neg-self-love which are your neg-emotions and the only UPS that exists for you.

Laws of Emotions

#1- Your own emotions+/- are the only Happiness ◇ UPS that exist for you.

Happiness and pain in life is very simple: it is your emotions+/-. Your emotions, positive◇negative, are the Happiness◇UPS polarity. Your negative emotions are the only pain and suffering that exist for you. On the Emotions Polarity Spectrum (next illustration): Happiness is the upper part; UPS the bottom.

2- Your Hap◇UPS in life is NEVER what occurs (events), but how you FEEL, your neg-emo.

Your emotions are your self-love+/- that you generate internally around the identities (PEIRs◇NEIRs) that you are activating in relation to the events.

The Emotions Polarity is the Happiness<>UPS Polarity

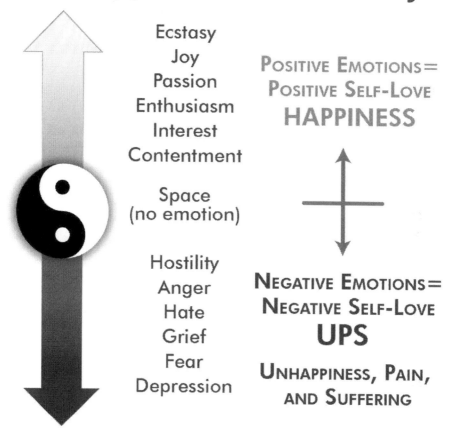

Ecstasy
Joy
Passion
Enthusiasm
Interest
Contentment

POSITIVE EMOTIONS=
POSITIVE SELF-LOVE
HAPPINESS

Space
(no emotion)

Hostility
Anger
Hate
Grief
Fear
Depression

NEGATIVE EMOTIONS=
NEGATIVE SELF-LOVE
UPS
UNHAPPINESS, PAIN,
AND SUFFERING

Your emotions are the only Happiness<>UPS that exist for you. Your Hap<>UPS is never what is or what occurs in your life (events), but how you FEEL about that. Furthermore, events are never the Cause of what you feel: your identities are.

Life is a parade of events. Your life has hundreds of events every day; just getting up is an event. Every interaction with another person is an event. Note that about most events, you have no emotions. For some events, you activate positive emotions (maybe you got recognition or a raise at work?) For others, you activate negative emotions (you got cut off in traffic or you lost your job, for examples).

Note that the events are external, physical experiences, sense perceptions. Note that your emotions are internal, non-physical experiences. There is no cause-effect relation between the two. You can have FEELings without events. And you can have events without feelings, which takes us to the next law:

#3- Events are never the Cause of your psycanic experience.

Events never create, generate,
what you FEEL, never cause your emotions:
neither negative (MODs) nor positive (MOPs).

External events neither cause your UPS nor can make you happy.

This understanding, called Responsability for Experience, is the make-break point for human beings between continuing to live in Drama and UPS, or transforming their lives to Power→Results. As long as a person operates in the paradigm, actually the hallucination, that external events cause his emotions, he has no hope of True Happiness. He will continue to live in the External Quest for happiness, which is impossible of success and so guarantees Victim, Game Conditions and DUPS.

One proof of this is that, for any given unvarying, external event, human emotional reactions vary along a spectrum from very negative to very positive. This violates Consistency of Cause.

Consistency of Cause

Consistency of Cause is one of the principles of science that you live every day. Consistency of Cause says that every Effect has its Cause and that every Cause *always* produces its Effects and *never* other Effects. For example, in the physical universe, if you give sugar, salt, and lemon juice to many people, all of them will report very similar experiences for each substance: sweet, salty, and sour. No one will say that sugar caused them sour, or salt caused them sweet. There is consistency of cause to effect, of substance to its particular flavor, and only its flavor.

Another example: If you put in one hand an ice cube and on the other drip hot wax, everyone will report consistency of hot and cold in their experience. No sane person will say ice causes hot and the wax is cold.

No one doubts that physical things cause physical experience, and that Consistency of Cause exists for the physical universe.

An example of Consistency of Cause is driving your automobile. You totally trust that your car will accelerate when you press the gas pedal; that turning the steering will turn the car in the same direction; and that pressing the brake pedal will slow and stop your vehicle. In fact, you bet your life on the absolute Consistency of Cause between the controls of your car and what the car does.

Imagine that there was no Consistency of Cause. One time you press the gas pedal and the car accelerates. But the next time you press it, the car turns right. Sometimes when you press the brake pedal, the car stops; but other times it accelerates or turns to one side or the other. Sometimes when you turn the steering wheel, the car turns in that direction, but sometimes it turns in the opposite direction, other times it stops and backs up.

Note how the physical universe would be chaos without Consistency of Cause. In fact, science itself is the observation and study of Effects to discern and understand their Causes so we can control them and produce the desired Effects (results). If there were no Consistency of Cause, there would be no science and we would have no control or prediction over the physical universe. We could not survive: some random, unpredictable effect would soon kill us, as would driving a car were there no Consistency of Cause.

Now, let's take our psycanic universes, our world of interior, trans-physical experience. Note that there is NO Consistency of Cause between anything in the physical universe and psycanic experience: thoughts and emotions. None.

Example: Take any person and asked the 20 people who know him/her best (the observers) what they think of that person. Their answers will range from very positive, even loving that person; to very negative, even to hating them. The 20 people will have different opinions (mental experiences) and degrees of emotional like<>dislike varying from very positive to very negative.

A good example in this year of 2020 is POTUS Donald Trump. At the positive end of the polarity spectrum of feelings about him are the people enchanted with him. On the negative end of the spectrum are all the people that despise and even hate him. And there are millions of people spread out at every point on the spectrum of love<>aversion between the two poles.

Another example: Some people grieve greatly when their mother or father dies. Others take it in stride with perhaps a little sadness. Some people are indifferent. Some people are glad (perhaps s/he abused them, or they are glad of the inheritance). The event "death of parent" does not cause the offspring's experience about it. It is the same event for everyone, but everyone's experience varies along a spectrum of experience that runs from great tragedy to satisfaction and celebration.

Another example: Some people are happy to divorce; for others it is traumatic.

Example: On September 11, 2001, terrorists crashed airliners into the two World Trade Towers in New York. For most Americans, this was a tragedy. But some people in other (usually Muslim) countries were dancing in the street. Same event, very different psycanic experiences. However, even in America there were different experiences. One NY gold trader on first hearing of the crash, thought "How horrible!" and in the next, went ecstatic as he thought about how gold prices would be soaring making him rich. Some people in neutral countries were indifferent to the event, and some expressed admiration for the cleverness of the attack without being happy about it.

Example: The crucifixion of Jesus: some people were for it, considering a triumph for good (their good, of course). They felt victorious. Others considered it bad, a loss and a tragedy, and felt sorrow and fear and went into hiding. Many people were indifferent. Again: same event: many different experiences.

In all examples mentioned, in any case you care to mention; there is no Consistency of Cause. Were there any Consistency of Cause, every observer would have the same experience about any given person /event, as observers do with tasting sugar and salt, etc. But the truth of life is that there are almost as many experiences (opinions and emotions) about any person or event as there are people observing / experiencing it.

Scientifically, **the cause of the variation of effect (the experience in the observers)** *must be* **in that which is varying,** the observers. The cause of the variation of effect (experience) **cannot be in that which is invariable**, not varying, i.e. the event. Thus, there is no relation of cause⬦effect between any event and psycanic experience about that event.

When the Cause is held constant, but the Effects vary, there is no causal connection between the two phenomena. For any event, human mental and emotional experiences will run the gamut from very negative to very positive. Ergo, there is no causal connection between events and psycanic experience.

Understanding all the above is critical to your happiness and your **Power to Discreate** your undesired realities and power to re-create your Self and your life. You can ONLY discreate realities you created, that are yours. If you believe that your psycanic realities (thoughts, emotions, identities, etc.) are created by anything other than yourself, you cannot discreate it. Victims cannot discreate.

To gain the power to discreate, you must make a paradigm shift from assigning Cause of your UPS to external events, to recognizing you are cause and creator of your psycanic experience. You must take on a state of BEing known as: **Acknowledgement of Creator** and **Responsability for Experience** (TT, (abbreviation **RespExp).** *(Note the spelling with an "a".)* RespExp (Responsability for Experience) means to recognize that you are the soul and sole creator of your psycanic experience, and to stop and assigning Cause to and blaming others and events for how you feel, for your MODs, for your UPS.

RespExp requires a transformation of paradigm from the **Fatal Identity** of "I am not cause; "I am not creator; I am not responsible for how I feel. I am the victim of events, of what others say and do and what happens in my life."

It is a change of your BEing to being At Cause: "I am the creator. I have the power. I decide Who I am, how I feel, and what I think. I am responsable for my emotions, not what others say or do, or what happens in my life.

Without this change, you will never have any power to discreate your negative realities. Without the power to discreate, you will never have very good results in creation, neither in in your psycanic world nor in your physical world. You cannot create positives over the top of negatives already present in your BEing; you must first discreate the negatives to create space for the positives.

All of this is so important, that we will have a complete chapter on it later in the second part of the book: Discreation.

What Does Cause My Emotions?

To understand what causes your emotions, you need to understand what your emotions really are. First, you do not have many different emotions. As we said before: Your emotions are a single energy polarity spectrum (just as temperature and visible light are). Your emotions are a single type of energy stretched between two poles of maximum negative emotion and maximum positive emotion.

On the positive side are all the positive emotions such as contentment, interest, satisfaction, enthusiasm, celebration, passion, and joy. These are the energies of happiness.

On the negative side are all the flavors of UPS which we can classify in the **Five Families** of negative emotions: anger, fear, sorrow or sadness, guilt, and depression.

1. Family of Anger: includes anger, frustration, impotence, resentment, rage, hate, etc.

2. Family of Fear: includes anxiety, worry, timidity, shyness, terror, panic, phobia, etc.

3. Family of Sadness: includes sadness, sorrow, grief, loneliness, etc.

4. Family of Guilt: includes guilt, remorse, regret, repentance, etc.

5. Family of Depression: includes depression, apathy, giving up, feeling defeated, powerlessness and hopelessness.

Your emotions are a single kind of energy stretched out into a polarity spectrum. Now we need to see exactly what kind of energy they are.

The Ultimate Nature of Emotion

Your emotions are your self-love.

**Your emotions+/- are your self-love+/-
energy polarity spectrum.**

**Love is a polarity, both love for self (FEEL)
and love for others (your DO).**

(All the Laws of Reality, Polarity, Love, and Happiness apply.)

_____

You an immortal spirit pretending to be human so you can live the Human Adventure Movie that is your life. Your positive emotions are part of you, of the spirit / you-psycan. They are the LJ, the Love-Joy, in your Divine Essence of WPVLJ. In Pure Essence, Essence outside of the Creation, there is no polarity and you are Absolute Love with no negative, no anti-love.

However, in the Creation we have Polarity including positive and negative love. **Your negative emotions are part of your anti-WPVLJ; they are your negative love for your Self.** Your neg-emo is the polar opposite of your WPVLJ Essence; it is anti-love for your Self. You created your negative emotions to help you explore **all that you are NOT in Essence**; to explore the opposite of your Essence, to explore self-anti-love and Drama-UPS. Remember, Drama is primarily the negative emotions we savor during a Game Conditions, which is to say that Drama is primarily negative self-love (for being in anti-power NEIRs.) This exploration of negatives is why you-psycan incarnated on Earth: to explore ALL THAT YOU ARE NOT IN ESSENCE. (This is an understanding from Essentiality.)

While Essence is Divine Bliss, to be experiencing only the 13 Characteristics (WPVLJ) ergo bliss for all eternity with no change is actually boring! (Imagine that you were sexing all day every day.) You have all eternity to explore ALL possibilities of experience, including the negatives. You have descended into the Creation to explore all possibilities of experience, especially the negative polarities.

The reason that your emotions are your Happiness<> UPS polarity is because Love (Divine Love) is the only true happiness that exists. Your **emotions+/- are that Love +/-.** As a psycan-individualization of Essence, part of your nature is BEing Divine Love. (All of this is from Essentiality, but you cannot truly understand your existence even as a human being without understanding your spiritual nature.)

To show that Love = Happiness, seek the answers to these questions in your experience (not in thought):

- Whom do you love? How does it feel to love? Happy or UPS?

- How does it feel to be loved? Happy or UPS?

- Have you ever been in love with a romantic partner? How happy were you "in love"? Did you "walk on air"?

- Do you love your children? Are not they joy in your life?

- Do you love at least one of your parents? How does that feel? Does it contribute to your happiness or your unhappiness in life?

Positive Love is Happiness.
Negative Love (neg-energy) is UPS.

Note how people after mystical experiences (including NDEs) report Light, Love and Joy (and other of the 13 Characteristics of Essence). When you open your BEing and learn to perceive Essence, it is difficult to even distinguish Love from Joy. (All students of the ESAE learn to open and feel Essence; She is around us everywhere all the time, Omnipresent. We are formed of Her. Our Essence is what we have blocked and counter-created to pretend to be human and explore anti-love, anti-power, Drama and UPS)

The next question is: What determines if your Love energy is positive (Joy / happy) or is negative (UPS)? I will express the answer in three ways varying the terminology to make the concept crystal-clear:

1- Your emotions+/- are your (divine) love energy+/- for your Self as determined by the Essence Identity+/- that you are (unconsciously) activating in relation to events.

2- Your emotions+/- are your self-love energy+/- determined by the PEIR <> NEIR that you are (unconsciously) choosing
and therefore BEing in relation to events.

3- Your emotions+/- are your self-love energy+/- for Who You Are BEing+/- which is determined by the PEIR <> NEIR that you are (unconsciously) assuming in relation to events.

All the above is the Causal Sequence in operation:

BE→ FEEL = [BE determines FEEL].

Identities → Emotions = [IDs determine emotions.]

- **Positive IDs (+BE) generate positive emotions = +FEEL = Happiness.**

- **Negative IDs (--BE-) generate negative emotions = UPS.**

To change your FEELings, change who you are BEing (your IDs).

We repeat the following because it is a critical understanding: Your own negative emotions are your only UPS in life. Your UPS is never the events, but how you FEEL about the events. And as we proved with Consistency of Cause, events never cause your emotions.

As long as you live assigning Cause to events, you are in the Fatal Identity Sequence, in No RespExp, and creating yourself the emotional victim of external events. Victims have no power to discreate their negative identities, no power over their experience, and only indirect power over their lives. (Indirect power is trying to change others to change one's experience: highly ineffective and generator of most problems in relationships.) Thus, Victims live in frequent, even constant, activations of their anti-power identities, and therefore in lots of DUPS. **IT IS IMPOSSIBLE TO BE A VICTIM AND HAPPY.** (We cover Victim in detail in a later chapter.)

You are the soul and sole creator of your emotions, ergo of your UPS or happiness in life. You cannot control your neg-emotions directly; suppression is not control and will cause physical health problems. You can try to suppress them with addictive substances and distracting activities, but you leave that mass of emotional energy in your subconscious. As long as that mass exists in your subconscious, it is subject to activation over and over again for the rest of your life. Without discreation of your causal NEIR, you have no permanent change in your BE-FEEL and therefore none in your Causal Sequences= life, nor in your Happiness<>UPS polarity experience. The world will continue to play emotional basketball with your FEELings.

You control your emotions by controlling your identities, by discreating your NEIRs and re-creating your Self as PEIRs. BTT (Being Transformation Technology) is a precision system for doing this.

Life is simple! It is:

$$BE \rightarrow FEEL \rightarrow THINK \rightarrow REL\text{-}DO \rightarrow HAVE$$

Your BEing determines your FEELings. Your identities+/- determine your emotions+/-. Your emotions are your self-love energy polarity spectrum, where the polarity of the emotion is determined by the polarity of your identities.

➢ Positive states of BEing (IDs) naturally produce positive emotions and positive results in life, ergo happiness.

➢ Negative states of BEing (IDs) perforce produce negative emotions, negative behaviors and poor results, and therefore Drama and UPS.

> Behind every positive emotion, there is a PEIR: you are loving yourself in that identity.

> Behind every negative emotion, there is a NEIR; you are anti-loving yourself for BEing anti-Essence with your neg-emo.

Self-Love means that you are loving your Self, you are feeling pos-emo about who you are BEing, your identity (PEIR) of the moment. **That Self-Love is the only True Happiness that exists.**

The secret of True Happiness is to first eliminate all your NEIRs which provoke your negative love to Self and are the only UPS that exists. Then re-create your BEing in PEIRs with will naturally activate your positive love for Self, your positive emotions which are the only happiness that exist.

- When your emotions are positive, you know that you are in a positive identity, a PEIR, which is activating your positive love for your Self, for your positive state of BEing.

- When your emotions are negative, you know that you are in a negative identity, a NEIR, which is activating your negative love for your Self in that negative State of BEing.

Celebrate this! When you are in neg-emo, you have the opportunity to use BTT to find and discreate your NEIR. The price of wasting opportunities is to prolong your UPS in life, to continue on the emotional roller coaster.

I take every opportunity to repeat these fundamental understandings about your existence, so here they are again:

#1- Your UPS in life is never what happens (i.e. your trigger events), but what you FEEL, your neg-emo, **around** the Identity you are activating in relation to the event.

#2- External events never cause your neg-emo=UPS; they only trigger into your experience your NEIR masses already present in your BEing (subconscious).

This is great news! because if they did cause your UPS, you would never be able to achieve happiness. If events cause our emotions, there would be no hope for human happiness because nobody, not even kings and emperors, has ever had the power to always control events, what others say and do, and what happens.

#3- *True Happiness = positive emotions all the time* begins when you have discreated your NEIR masses to thereby eliminate all your MOD activations of neg-emo=UPS. You are then naturally PEIRs which automatically trigger your love for Self, which are the positive emotions, which are happiness.

Corollary to #2: Just as external events are never the cause of your neg-emo=UPS, positive external events can never produce your happiness. They come and go. Even when they stay awhile, the positive emotions (MOP) fades away. For example: how long does the pos emo charge of getting a new car last? How long does falling in love last? How long do you celebrate a raise or a promotion at work?

Furthermore, as long as you still have your NEIR mass, events will activate them and will overpower your MOP. Your True Happiness cannot depend on anything outside of you because "Change is the only Constant". For your Happiness to be permanent, constant, and impregnable to events, it must be something you create and control within you.

#4 - Every activation of your **NEIR masses→neg-emo** is a critical moment. You have Two Paths:

A- **The Lo Road**: block, suppress, drug, or ignore it, and the mass will eventually subside back into your subconscious such that you are no longer experience it in present time. The problem is that your mass continues in existence ready to trigger again at any moment. **YOU MAKE NO PROGRESS IN CLEANING YOUR BEING OF NEGATIVE ENERGY.**

B- **The Hi Road:** Discreate the NEIR upon which the mass dissolves and you return to positive experience AND your subconscious Space of BEing is permanently free of that quantity of the total neg-energy in your BEing. (As a human being, you have a lot of neg-energy.) You are forever free of that NEIR mass. Repeat this on every activation and eventually you will have no activations. Your PEIRs + pos-emotion will then dominate your experience and your Causal Sequences.

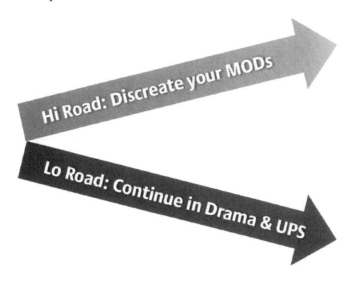

Hi Road: Discreate your MODs

Lo Road: Continue in Drama & UPS

Summary:

1- Behind every negative emotion, there is <u>always</u> a negative ID (NEIR). ALWAYS, no exceptions. (BE causes FEEL; your emotions are your self-love energy determined by who you are BEing at the moment.

2- Our objective is that you learn to penetrate any negative emotion to find — *in experience, not in mind!* — your causal NEIR, your negative BE.

3- Once you experiencing your NEIR, you can discreate it using BTT.

4- You then re-create yourself in your ideal of who you want to BE, in PEIRs that affirm your WPVLJ.

5- That Causal Sequence will then change with a minimal energization of what you then want to experience in each Arena.

As your BEing (identities) are the initial and only true causal element in your Causal Sequences, transforming your BEing from negative to positive will automatically change the other Arenas of your life starting with your FEEL, your happiness.

The core of how to do this is:

1- FEEL into your negative emotion to find your CAUSAL NEIR(s).

2- DISCREATE that NEIR with BTT which permanently eliminates it from your BEing and will automatically eliminate your neg-emo activation. (Part 2 of this book is how to discreate.)

3- RE-CREATE your Self (your BEing) in the appropriate PEIR, which will automatically produce *positive emotion = happiness.* (Creation is last part of this book.)

4- WATCH the MAGIC: that Causal Sequence will transform to positive in all your other arenas: THINK, RELATE, DO, and HAVE.

The full 14-step protocol for BTT is in a coming chapter.

The Impossible Dream of the External Quest is trying to control externals to stop our negative experience (MODs and UPS) – which leads to the Don Quixote Behaviors of trying to control others to stop them from triggering our MODs; and to all addictions.

Your relationship problems result because you are trying to control (avoid, stop) your neg-emo-UPS by changing the outside world – and usually with neg-energy, which others will resist, defend themselves, and counter-attack you.

The power of your addictions over your is the power of your Existential Imperative to escape pain (by suppressing your negative psycanic experience with chemicals).

When you learn to control your emotions (by discreating their NEIR masses), you will be able to control your negative behaviors (for examples: addictions and relationship conflicts). By controlling your BEing, you will be able to control your THINK, RELATE, DO and HAVE easily.

Addendum on Self-Love versus Love for Others

It is critical to the quality of your relationships to understand love-for-self versus love-for-others. Love is a polarity, both self-love and love for others. Positive love is all forms of positive energy and actions that contribute to the well-being of others and the world.

Negative love, aka anti-love, aka evil, is all forms of negative energy and actions that lower energy or organization, that harm, destroy, cause suffering or injustice.

Your love for your Self is your emotions, your FEEL in the Causal Sequence. Positive emotions are positive self-love and happiness. Negative emotions are negative self-love and UPS.

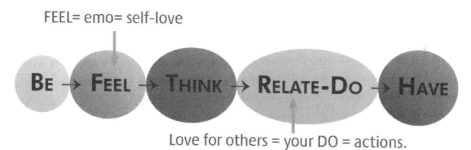

FEEL= emo= self-love

BE → FEEL → THINK → RELATE-DO → HAVE

Love for others = your DO = actions.

Your love for others is your DO in the Causal Sequence (your RELATE). Others don't experience how you FEEL; they experience what you DO, how you treat them. Your love, positive or negative, for others is the **energy**, positive or negative, that you give them, use with them. Your love for others is how you communicate and deal with them. It is your integrity and honesty with them. It is whether your actions contribute to and grow their well-being and the quality of their lives, or whether your actions and behaviors decrease their aliveness and happiness.

(Common examples of anti-love in relationships: invalidation, judgement, criticism, hostility, anger, resentment, spite, manipulation, victim, domination/control, blaming and guilting, disapproval, withdrawing affection or support, conflicts and arguments, cold shoulder, recriminations, punishment, withholding sex, to name a few.)

Notice that your emotions, i.e. your feelings, **are irrelevant** as to whether you love or anti-love others. You can be angry with someone (your negative self-love) and still treat them with love: with Space, patience, compassion, and support. You can profess to love someone and still treat them with negative energy, in which case your "love" is a lie. The truth is you are anti-loving them. (Space is the absence of all negative energy; it is acceptance and the beginning of love.)

Others don't feel your love, your feelings. They may not even know how you feel. And if you are treating them with anti-love, won't care. They don't experience your emotions; they experience the energy and behaviors with which you deal with them. What they experience is whether your actions increase or decrease their energy. That is your love or anti-love for others, not how you FEEL.

How you FEEL has nothing to do with your love for others -- unless you let it dictate how you treat them, i.e. negatively when you are activated. Again: do not confuse self-love, your emotions, how you FEEL, with True Love for others. To do so will impossibilitate True Love in your relationships. True Love is an act of will; it is your commitment to always give Space to others to BE as they are and Not-BE as they are not. It is your commitment expressed in your positive actions to care for, teach, and grow the energies around you.

When you feel love for others, i.e. positive emotions, it is really your love for your Self that you activating because you are BEing a PEIR in relation to them as an external event. If that love is not a creation out of your will impregnable to your negative emotions, it is only a MOP, the external activation of a PEIR mass.

Your love is only True Love when it is your creation of PEIRs and love all the time no matter what, and expresses in your actions to only treat others with positive energy, no matter what you FEEL. When most people say, "I love you", what they are really saying is: "**You tickle my PEIRS** and make me feel good, so I must 'love' you". Not much True Love in that.

It is easy to love others when they are giving you positive energy and you are feeling good. Where you really see whether you have the Power of BEing to Truly Love, to Divinely Love, is how you behave when others are giving you negative energy, giving you anti-love. Can you receive negative love from others and always respond with space, transparency, serenity, and positive energy?

Our great example of this is, of course, Jesus, who at his crucifixion faced the maximum and most painful anti-love the planet had invented, and remained in Space and forgiveness, in positive energy = Love.

Compare that with how most humans get angry, even enraged, at even small perceived slights (one example is road rage). As humans, our untrained capacity to love, to love when receiving anti-love, neg-energy, is slight.

16- NEIR Masses

Your identities and emotions are bundled together in NEIR masses. A NEIR mass is an agglomeration of psycanic energy with various elements. The four most important components are:

1- A NEIR (Negative Essence Identity Reality).

2- Resistance to the NEIR, result of the opinion of Bad-SNB (TT) to it.

3- Negative emotion (neg self-love = neg-emo = UPS).

4- Negative THINK: determinations and programs (Book III).

However, all the possible components include:

1. Various NEIRs.

2. **Resistance** to BE-FEELing the NEIR.

3. One or more **opinions of Bad-SNB** to the NEIR.

4. Opinions of Bad-SNB to the trigger event or person.

5. Negative emotion energy, which is both self-anti-love and resistance to the NEIR and neg-energy to attack the trigger event / person (to stop, change, punish, or destroy it).

6. Other negative THINK creations such as invalidations, criticisms, judgements, determinations and programs (very important).

Illustration: A NEIR Mass Identity Reality
with its four main components.

A NEIR Mass Identity Reality with its four main components.

1. The **NEIR** itself, a mass of energy forming a reality-identity about Self.

2. The **Opinion of Bad-SNB** to the NEIR, which generates **Resistance** to BE-FEELing the NEIR (which stops Experience and therefore discreation).

3. The **neg-FEEL = neg-emo charge** (anger, anxiety, fear, sadness, guilt, etc.)

4. Negative **THINK**: invalidations, determinations, programs, judgments, etc.

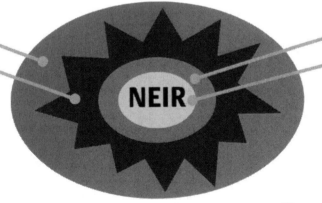

When the components are not important, we will represent a NEIR mass with just a negative star:

Your NEIR masses sit latent in your subconscious until a trigger event occurs, upon which you (unconsciously) assume a NEIR in relation to that event. For example, your boss assigns you a big project at work. You may go into the power identity of, "Yes, I can do it!" in which case your self-love-emo will be positive, such as gusto, excitement or enthusiasm. Or you may go into an anti-power identity, a NEIR, of, "I can't do this"; I am unable; I am incapable" or similar. In this case of a NEIR, your self-love-emo will be negative: anxiety, worry, fear, anger, frustration, impotence, desperation, etc.

Your unwitting activation of an anti-power identity, of BEing that NEIR, will pull the entire NEIR mass from your subconscious into you-psycan-consciousness-experience. Again, you may experience your activation (MOD) primarily as the negative emotion, but the NEIR is always there, no exceptions.

You-psycan activate, assume, an Essence ID (WPVLJ) <u>in relation to the trigger event</u>. Your ID is who are BEing in handling that event: for example: powerful or not-powerful. That identity will be either positive or negative (PEIRs or NEIR). Everything else in your Causal Sequence unfolds from that identity, your BE. PEIRs produce positive causal sequences across all Arenas. NEIRs produce negative causal sequences across all Arenas. We will see this in depth for the rightmost Arenas, THINK, RELATE, DO, and HAVE in Book III. In this book I, we are interested in the BE→FEEL and you being able to penetrate your FEEL, your neg-emo to find your NEIR in your experience, not in thought/mind.

$$BE \text{ (determines)} \to FEEL, \text{THINK, RELATE, DO, HAVE}$$

The Four NEIRs:

Although there are dozens of ways to name a NEIR or to describe it using words, there are only four flavors. Each is a polarity.

1. **Wisdom**: You are intelligent and wise enough to handle the event; OR you are unintelligent, ignorant, or stupid in relation to the event.

2. **Power**: You are {able<>unable} to handle the trigger event.
   You are {capable <> incapable} of producing your desired results. You are {powerful<>not powerful} in dealing with the situation.
   You are {strong<>weak} in relationship to the event.
   You are a {success<>failure} in that area of your life.

3. **Value**: You are valuable, worthy, and deserving in relationship to the event; OR you are not valuable; you are unworthy or undeserving, in relation to the event.

4. **Love**: You are a good<>bad person in relation to the event, and therefore you are lovable or unlovable. (This fourth NEIR is any form of "I am a bad person" in whatever role, personal or commercial. Examples of personal roles: spouse, parent, son, daughter, grandchild. Examples of commercial roles: lawyer, doctor, secretary, carpenter, etc.).

We repeat because this is so critical in understanding all human experience and behavior: **When a trigger event occurs, you subconsciously "recall" from your subconscious an identity, a NEIR, in relation to that event.** The identity jumps in on you-consciousness bringing with it the entire NEIR mass, all its components. **You experience your NEIR mass mostly as negative emotion (UPS), but the NEIR is always there** inside of the emotion.

The movement of the NEIR mass from your subconscious to your consciousness is called an "**activation**", aka a "**MOD**", a **Moment of Dolor** (Dolor is Latin for pain). The mechanism we explain in the next chapter.

The opposite polarity of a NEIR mass MOD is the assumption of a positive Essence identity, a PEIR in relation to an event. This activates the movement of a PEIRs mass, a PEIR plus its emo charge of positive self-love, from your subconscious to your experience. PEIR activations are also called MOPs: Moment of Pleasure. MOPs are the cherries of life, to be enjoyed: the problem enters when people mistake them for happiness and waste their lives chasing them instead of working on their BEing to achieve True Happiness.

Again, because of its extreme importance, because it is the make-break point of the human being between living in Victim and Drama, versus moving to Power and Happiness:

Trigger events do not create or cause negative emotions. They only stimulate into consciousness NEIR masses created long ago -- usually in childhood we tell beginner explorers in psycanics, although the truth is they are part of your human identity Shell, which you-psycan created before incarnating. **The purpose of their creation is to counter-create your spiritual nature of WPVLJ so you can explore Game Conditions and Drama.**

Understand: Every time you experience an activation / MOD you are not experiencing *newly-created-in-the-moment* **neg-emo. NO! You are experiencing the same NEIR and the same emo-energy charges over and over and over again.** They are the same masses being triggered into your perception and then subsiding back into your subconscious (out of perception) over and over again. They will continue to do this until you discreate the mass – which is exactly what BTT does.

You-psycan have a limited number of PEIR masses, each with a limited amount of charge.

Your NEIR masses that you do not discreate, when the opportunity of their activation presents itself, will eventually subside back into your subconscious, often aided by addictive substances and distractor activities. They will remain latent in your subconsciousness, awaiting the next trigger.

Your NEIR Masses will keep moving back and forth from your subconscious to your consciousness until you discreate them.

(Notice how you have been living the same MODs, the same NEIR mass experiences and some emotions, over and over again. The triggers are as infinitely variable as is life, but your NEIR masses are the same ones "vibrating" back and forth between your subconsciousness and your consciousness-experience. Remember, you have 4 main masses, the 4 NEIRs. Each has sub masses and maybe a dozen variations. It is a lot of ECRE, but it is not even close to infinite.

To the ordinary human being operating in the Fatal Identity Sequence, it seems that the trigger events are causing his MODs. But this is an illusion, a hallucination -- as is the Fatal Identity. The person is carrying around his NEIR Masses with him all the time, everywhere he goes. Events only trigger what is always there (until discreated). All this we will see in the next chapter.

Causal Sequence: BE determines FEEL

• Positive identities (PEIRs) generate positive emotions (+FEEL).
If you are in pos-emo, you are in a PEIR.

• Negative identities (NEIRs) generate negative emotions (UPS).
If you are in neg-emo, you are in a NEIR. (Discreate it!)

• All neg behaviors (DO) are intents to stop your neg BE-FEEL and produce positive BE-FEEL. Examples of neg-DO to control BE-FEEL include addictions and relationship conflicts.

• Change your BE and your FEEL will automatically change, and it is easy to change your RELATE, DO, and HAVE.

To transform your entire life, transform who you are BEing by discreating all your NEIRs and re-creating your Self in PEIRs.

17- Activations / MODs

How Your NEIR Mass Activations Work

In this chapter, we examine in depth where your negative emotions come from and how they work. You will have noticed that they come and go, in and out of your experience; you have daily, even hourly, MOD activations. Your negative emotions are one element of your NEIR masses residing in your subconscious. They are **negative self-love resistances** to who you are, to your BE, when you are in a NEIR.

This chapter is the how and why of their travels from your subconscious to your consciousness and back. It also introduces the solution to eliminating your neg-emo forever. Once free of negative emotions, and having learned to maintain your Self in PEIRs all the time, you will naturally live in the upper, positive part of the emotional spectrum: True Happiness. Your lowest moments will be peace and serenity; your higher moments in life: passion and joy.

It only takes an hour or two of correctly piloted BTT to eliminate the negative emotion associated with any particular trigger. As we mentioned before, it takes about 400 hours of BTT to eliminate permanently all your negative human[1] emotions.

---

[1] Human emotions: We include "human" here because you-psycan also have negative energies from a higher, spiritual level of your BEing, which level is explained in Essentiality.

Conscious <> Subconscious

You are consciousness; you are formed of consciousness. You are a sphere or globe of consciousness (as well as all the other Characteristics of Essence: it is all One Energy). Your consciousness is a field of energy which detects, perceives, experiences, other energies (realities). You might think of it as a spider web that vibrates when an insect lands on it. You can also think of it as the screen of your computer or cell phone, blank until energy signals arrive from the programming to put images and information (realities) on the screen.

Your subconscious is the psycanic space around you-psycan in which your ECRE are outside of your present-time perception. (Reminder: Your psycanic ECRE include your identities, emotions, thoughts, memories, motivations to behavior, relationship energies, etc., and above all: your NEIR masses.)

Illustration: Psycan, Conscious, and Subconscious

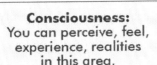

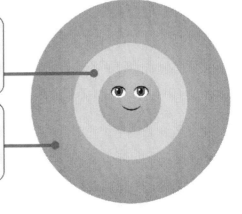

Activations

Your activations occur when a trigger event activates a NEIR mass into your experience. Your activations are Moments of Pain (abbreviated: MOD). MODs are your periods, "fits" or "attacks", of negative emotions, of UPS. (The activation of positive emotion (self-love for BEing a PEIR), are called MOPs, Moments of Pleasure. However, unless specified as a MOP, an activation always refers to the activation of a NEIR mass, a MOD.

- MOD: Moment of Dolor=Pain: activation of a NEIR mass.

- MOP: Moment of Pleasure: activation of a PEIR mass.

Definition: An **activation** is the triggering and movement of a NEIR mass from your subconscious (out-of-perception), to your conscious-experience, to your FEELing. An activation is the jump of a NEIR with all its surrounding elements from your subconscious into your consciousness where you experience it primarily as negative emotions, as UPS. A synonym for an activation is MOD. Life as recurring MODs is the essence of Drama and UPS.

Although you may only be feeling or aware of the negative emotion, **the NEIR is always present** inside the neg-emo. If your neg-emo is very strong, you may not perceive the NEIR as its perception can be drowned out by the quantity and intensity of the emotion.

**Inside of all neg-emo = MODs= UPS,
there are always NEIRs.**

NO KNOWN EXCEPTIONS.

Your activation is your NEIR plus your neg love for to your Self for being that NEIR. NEIR masses are latent in your subconscious, and any negative event (from your perspective) can trigger them into your experience.

Jellos are people who feel easily; who are very emotional. They tend to be impulsive in their behaviors and to live in Victim.

Rock are people who have their feelings (emotions) shut down to some extent. They tend to be mental and "cold" compared to Jellos. Rocks may have trouble finding their NEIRs because they have their feeling blocked and only strong emotions get through. We will explain jellos and rocks in later chapters.

Our objective always is to penetrate the neg-emo, find the NEIR, discreate it, and re-create our BEing in PEIRs. Repeat this on every activation, and eventually you will have no more NEIRs and therefore no more neg-emo.

Illustration: Activation, aka MOD.

An event occurs and the psycan assumes an identity, a state of BEing, in relation to the event. The identity creation-reality (NEIR) moves from the subconscious into experience bringing with it all its other elements, particularly self-love+/-.

Activation, aka MOD.

Any Trigger Event

An activation (MOD) is the movement of a NEIR Mass from your subconscious (out-of-perception)→ to your consciousness= perception= feeling.

"Bad" external events can trigger NEIR Masses to jump from subconscious to conscious but they never create or cause them.

What to Discreate

It is the NEIR that you must discreate, not the neg-emo. To discreate the NEIR, you will have to discreate all resistance to BE-FEELing the NEIR, which can be done by Exp2 on the Rxx, or by discreating Bad-SNB (which is the creation that triggers the Rxx). Again, a chapter is coming on this.

Discharging and discreating negative emotions is generally a waste of TE. You can discharge emotion by experiencing it out without discreating the NEIR. However, if you don't discreate the NEIR, the emotion will regenerate itself because it is your neg-self-love for BEing the NEIR. On discreating the NEIR, the neg-emo will disappear by itself.

There are special BTT situations where a pilot will send the explorer to experience emotions, but there is always a specific reason. For example, in the Psycanics' BTT Course, "rock" students focus in emotions to rehabilitate their capacity to open to and feel negative energy without resistance.

Event, External Event

The word "event" is used very generally. An event is any change or movement of anything in your world, any occurrence. It can be something someone says or does. It can be a person or thing entering or leaving your life (e.g. arrival of in-laws, divorce, death, losing money). It can be even be a static situation or a circumstance (having debts, infidelity of your spouse, not having a job).

Trigger Event, Trigger.

A trigger is any event in your life which activates your NEIR masses, ergo your negative emotions. Anything can be a trigger: a person, an occurrence, a situation, a thought. Triggers can be **external,** such as something someone says or does; or **internal**: our own thoughts and memories can activate us. (Note: A positive event can trigger a PEIR mass, that is, a MOP, but unless specified as positive, "trigger" will always mean a NEIR mass trigger.)

How Triggers Work

Whenever a negative event occurs -- for example someone says or does something you don't like -- you unconsciously assume an identity, a NEIR, in relation to the event. At the speed of unconscious thought (i.e. almost instantly), your NIER mass moves in on you and you suffer its neg self-love-emo charge. This is happening over and over as you go through life.

For example, you enter a new social situation. Meeting new people, especially if you judge that they are better than you in some way, can trigger anti-value NEIRs such as: "I am not good enough *(smart enough, powerful enough, rich enough – whatever)*; I am less than; I am worth less; I am small; I am unimportant; I am invisible; I don't matter much", etc. You will experience uncomfortable emotions such as shyness, fear of rejection, self-doubt, lack of confidence, feeling out of place, even sadness or loneliness (even amid a crowd).

Another example: you approach someone and are rebuffed or rejected. You activate in the same anti-value NEIRs as: I am not good enough; I am less than others: I am unworthy. Your neg-self-love-emo will be sadness, loneliness, perhaps shame. These identities stop men from approaching women and are the root of all jealousy.

Triggers Appear to Cause MODs

To a person living in the **Fatal Identity Sequence** (I am not the creator of my experience; external things causes my feelings), who is therefore in no-responsability for his experience; it _appears_ that the trigger causes his MOD / UPS. The trigger event occurs and his negative emotions appear, over and over again. Naturally, he associates cause-effect to that sequence of events.

He perceives:

Trigger → MOD → assumption: external events cause my UPS.

What he does not understand is that between the trigger and his neg-emo, there stands him Self, his BEing, his identities, his NEIRs. What he does not understand is that his Point of Power, of control and change, is his identities, not the events, and not his emotions. You can't do much about your negative emotions directly (except suppression and drugs which are unhealthy). Your neg-emotions are your automatic self-love responses to your neg-identities (NEIRs). What you can control are your identities; these you can create and discreate at will

We emphasize: We say *"appear"* because events never, ever, cause your psycanic experience. It is impossible that something external creates or causes you any internal, psycanic experience. Impossible. Your identities determine your emotions: BE→FEEL; never your HAVE, the events in your life. Events only trigger your NEIRs with their masses of negative emotion. Your NEIR masses are your creations and always present in your subconscious until you discreate them.

Your neg-emotions are charges of neg self-love energy that you have created around your neg-BEing (NEIRs). Your NEIR masses are psycanic energies that you carry around with you in your subconsciousness all the time and everywhere you go. The true sequence of events is:

Trigger → NEIR ← neg-emo

Your Point of Power is the NEIR.

You can never stop all triggers, nor can you control neg-emo directly.

Your triggers in life may be many and varied, but observe that your feelings are the same emotional charges over and over again. And they will continue to activate over and over again until you discreate the NEIR. As long as the NEIR masses exist in your subconscious, they will always be sensitive to activation by negative events. As Life itself is a Polarity with positive and negative events (*from any human point of view*), you can depend on life to always supply you with trigger events if you have NEIRs available.

The key to magical power over life is to discreate your NEIRs which dissipates their masses of emotional energy. If you have no NEIR, there is nothing there to trigger. You will live in serenity and peace no matter the external events. From that serenity and peace, you will have more wisdom and more love to handle effectively the external situations.

MOPs

The reverse is true for MOPs, Moments of Pleasure, which are the activation of your PEIRS and positive self-love. For example, you win a bet or at poker or a sports match, or complete a project at work. In relation to that event, you unconsciously assume a PEIR such as: **"I did it; I am a winner; I am powerful; I am a success"**. Positive identities will always be accompanied by positive self-love which are the positive emotions: satisfaction, enthusiasm, celebration, joy, etc.

If you were free of all NEIR masses, ergo of MODs and UPS, and so living in PEIRs by your creation and all the time, you would be in True Happiness.

We cannot consider MOPs happiness when the BEing is in the External Quest seeking and depending on external events to produce, to trigger their positive experience (MOPs). There are several reasons for this:

#1- There is no real cause, control, decision, creation, and maintenance by the BEing of Who She Is. She is living at the effect of external events and depending on external events to generate her experience.

#2- A person who has not done the internal discreation work necessary to eliminate his NEIRs will have them all his life. They will continue to activate and the resulting MODs overpower and wipeout MOPs.

#3- No one has the power to so control the world as to make life a steady stream of only positive triggers→MOPS. Controlling the world to be happy is the Impossible Dream.

#4- MOPs don't last long. Just as MODs eventually subside back into the subconscious, so do MOPs. Think of several MOPs you have achieved, things you thought would make you happy long term. How long did they last? For example, how long does the pleasure of a new car last? Most people say less than three months, dying out day by day.

A person in True Happiness can maintain her experience of BEing PEIRs no matter what happens in her world. <u>She has stopped letting events "decide" who she is.</u> She consciously creates and control Who She Is, PEIRS. She consciously holds her positive identities in the face of the world, of all negative trigger events.

> ## MOPs
> ### MOMENTS OF PLEASURE
> MOPs are the activation of a PEIR Mass with its positive self-love emotion by a positive trigger event. MOPs are not True Happiness because:
> 1- The person is depending on externals to feel good (External Quest); and
> 2- As long as he has NEIRs, they will continue to be triggered making the MOPs short-lived.

Positive Event triggers PEIR Mass

Revision of Definitions

UPS: Unhappiness, Pain, and Suffering

Your only UPS in life is your activations of your NEIR masses with their neg-emo (MODs). Your UPS is never the events, but your neg-id-emo activations about those events. Events never cause your activations; your NEIRs do.

MOD: Moments of Dolor

MOD is the abbreviation for **Moments of Dolor** (Dolor is Latin for pain). **MOD is a synonym for an activation.** A MOD, an activation, is the hop of a NEIR mass from your subconscious into your consciousness where you experience it as negative emotion, as pain, as dolor, as UPS. A MOD exists all the time that a person is experiencing negative mental and emotional energy. MOD activations can last from a few seconds to hours, to days, in some cases, years (e.g. grieving for the death of a child or resentment over a divorce). BTT can end any MOD is a few hours by discreating the NEIRs behind it.

MOP: Moments of Pleasure

MOP is the abbreviation for Moments of Pleasure. A MOP is the opposite of a MOD. MOPs are the activations of positive emotions (self-love) that we enjoy when we achieve some goal or pleasurable experience (sex, success, money, vacations, traveling, a raise at work, marrying, divorcing, etc.). A MOP is the activation of a PEIR mass with its positive emotions that you experience when life presents you with a positive event trigger, and you assume BEing a PEIR in relation to that event.

MOPs exist because positive events and achievements activate our PEIRs of BEing intelligent, capable (powerful), valuable, or good (WPVLJ). PEIRs are naturally accompanied by the positive self-love that are the positive emotions (just as NEIRs are always accompanied by neg self-love).

The great problem with MOPs is that people mistake them for happiness. MOPs are the **mirage** of happiness, not True Happiness. They then go into the **External Quest**, the **Impossible Dream** of achieving True Happiness by accumulating MOPs: material possessions and properties, relationships, success, wealth, fame, power. *(We will see the External Quest in a later chapter.)*

As we mentioned above, MOPs are not True Happiness because they depend on external triggers, and therefore are not under the control of the BEing. They come and go as our fortunes vary, as we get or don't get what we want. MOPs are always **fleeting**; they always pass, either fading away in an hour, a day or a week, or blown away by the next MOD. (How long did your MOP last the when you graduated from school, got your first job, or got a raise?)

True Happiness is all the time, no matter what happens in life. It is a state of positive emotions (ergo self-love) all the time. It is independent and free of external conditions. It is not affected by triggers; it is free of activations / MODs.

True Happiness is a state of BEing, of being PEIRs all the time. Such a person has discreated all his NEIRs, ergo he has no activations, no MODs, no UPS. He has no NEIR masses bar events to trigger. Thus, he lives in self-love-joy all the time, irrelevant of what occurs in his life. He needs nothing outside of himself to be happy all the time and is not affected identically-emotionally (BE-FEEL) by negative events.

In True Happiness, the psycan has discreated all his NEIRs and can maintain his PEIR identities no matter what situations (triggers) life presents. His PEIRs→Happiness is totally self-contained.

A person who does not understand the difference between MOPs and True Happiness will waste his TE (Time and Energy) pursuing and accumulating MOPs instead of working on himself with BTT to create True Happiness. As mentioned above, that external pursuit of happiness is called the External Quest and, as it is impossible of success., also called the "Impossible Dream".

MOPs are not bad or wrong; they are to be enjoyed. However, they should not be mistaken for Happiness and never be the center of your life: they are ultimately empty and fleeting experiences compared to True Happiness.

Examples of common MOPs:
- Parties or hanging out with friends.
- Drinking
- Drugs
- Travel
- Shopping
- Vacations
- Falling in love
- Getting married

Important: MOPs are not bad or wrong; they are to be enjoyed. They are the cherries of life. The problem enters when a person mistakes them for happiness and centers his life in chasing and achieving MOPs (which is how UHBs live). People pursue MOPs in the illusion that one day they will finally be happy when they get **_enough_** of the **_right_** things (whatever they believe will produce their happiness). The **_right_** thing, the Golden Ring of the Merry-Go-Round of the External Quest, varies from person to person. Common "happiness" targets are relationships, marriage, family, children, sex, career success, money, material possessions and properties, fame, power.

The External Quest also keeps the person on the roller coaster of "Never-Enough-ness". As nothing external can ever produce True Happiness, a person in the External Quest will never be satisfied for long. The MOP will pass and he return to feeling the background dissatisfaction of all UHB life, the feeling that something is lacking, even complete emptiness. No matter how much a person in the External Quest achieves of fame and fortune, he will always feel that it is not enough, that he needs more. Nothing external can ever fill the emptiness within.

— —-

Laws of Psycanics

Activations destroy Wisdom.
Lack of Wisdom destroys Power.
Lack of Wisdom destroys Love.
Lack of Power impossibilitates Love.

Without Wisdom and Love guiding Power, Power destroys.
Without Wisdom to guide it, Love destroys.

(Definition: Power: your ability to produce your desired results.)

When you are activated, you are in a NEIR. You will THINK and DO, decide and act, from your negative state of BE. Negative BE naturally produces neg - THINK (anti-wisdom) and neg-DO, and these naturally produce negative results, neg-HAVE.

You have experienced this law many times. Have you ever tried to argue reason with a person in anger or in fear? How many times have you regretted something that you said or did when you were angry? How many times have you let fear stop you from taking action? How often do people let greed or fear affect their investment decisions?

Law: **Without Wisdom, both Love and Power destroy.**

Without the guidance of wisdom, both love and power destroy. This law we also see in operation every day. How many parents, in the name of love, spoil their children such that their as adults are irresponsible, or can't hold a job, or become alcoholics or drug addicts? How many people, with the best of intentions, enter relationships with insufficient understanding of love to make them work? (The divorce rate in the US is currently about 50%.) Note: True Love in relationships is nothing like what most people believe it is: it requires Wisdom. (We will present the Laws of True Love in the psycanics books on relationships.)

This law also applies to positive activations. A great example is when people "fall in love", when they are infatuated with each other. In the heat of their emotion, they make the great mistake of getting married, only to eventually divorced. "In love" is an activation, a positive one, a MOP, but an activation nonetheless. All activations, **positive or negative**, cause turbulence in the mind and destroy wisdom and therefore the power to produce the desired results.

If you are "in love" enjoy it all that you can, but don't make any long-term commitments until the emotion passes. It is not wise to marry a person you are infatuated with as long as you are in that activation. Your activation is actually self-love because you are assuming a PEIR in relation to that person. You feel wise, powerful, valuable, love, appreciated in relationship. The love you are FEELing and attributing to the other person is really love for yourself in your positive identities. Remember, love for self is how you FEEL; love for other is what you DO, how you treat them: with positive energy=love, or with negative energy= neg-love.

Who you should look to marry is your best friend. You want to marry a person who knows the worst about you and still accepts and loves you. You want to marry a person whom you can trust to keep their word and agreements. You want to marry a person with whom you have values and goals in common. You want to be and to marry someone who can love out of their will to do so, not out of how they feel at the moment.

If you are "in love" with someone, enjoy it to the fullest -- but don't make any long-term decisions based on your emotions until you have eliminated your negative ones. Humans come with bundles of NEIR masses and are in the External Quest to control them. Marriage increases triggers. Two bundles of NEIR masses triggering each other usually results in a relationship that spirals downward into more and more reactivity and neg energy until the only solution appears to get away from each other, i.e. divorce. People free of NEIR masses, SEBs, have relationships naturally free of neg-emo, of reactivity; they live in serenity, harmony, love, and cooperation.

Furthermore, your infatuation is not with the other person; it is with your Self BEing the PEIRs you are activating in relationship to that person. Until you take control of your BEing, discreate your NEIR and re-create yourself in PEIRs, your experience, emotions and Happiness<>UPS will always be at the effect of external events (in this case the person you are infatuated with). Infatuated, you get married as part of your External Quest trying to maintain your positive experience by keeping that person close to you. This does not work as evidenced by the 50% divorce percentage and that 40% of the other 50% stay together but in negative-energy, unhappy relationships.

End of Chapter

18- Your Two Paths

There are two ways, two paths, by which you can handle your negative psycanic experience, your MODs and UPS.

Path #1- How the UHB (Unenlightened Human Being) in the Fatal Identity Sequence and Drama perceives and reacts to life:

Trigger → causes my UPS.

Solutions: (None of which work to produce happiness)

A- Attack the trigger with neg energy to change, stop, punish, or destroy it and so end my MOD and prevent future ones. This causes conflicts in relationships.

B- Suppress my negative experience with substances or distractor activities.

Both are External Quest.

External Quest includes:

A.   attack trigger person to change, stop or punish him; or

B.   ingest chemicals (meds or illegal drugs);

C.   suppress UPS with other addictive substances;

D.   use distractor activities, which also become addictions;

E.   seek a MOP to feel better.

F.   all the above.

Your External Quest solution may work to change your experience for the moment, but it does nothing for you long term as you are leaving the causal NEIR mass intact.

Path #2 - How an SEB (Spiritually Enlightened BEing) understands and operates his life.

Trigger → stimulates my NEIRs → producing my UPS.
I am the creator and only person responsible for my UPS.

Solution:

1. Thank the trigger for showing me where to work on my Self.

2. Discreate my NEIRs and energize my Self in PEIRs.

3. Enjoy my resulting self-love- joy.

4. Repeat with each activation until I no longer have NEIRs & MODs and my BEing is pure PEIRs and love-joy.

— —-

Every time you are activated, you stand at a fork in the road of your happiness. You have two paths: External Quest or BTT. You can resist your experience and suppress the activation, or you can discreate it by discreating the NEIR.

Which one you choose is critical to your happiness.

Path #1: You can ignore the activation and go into Negative DO of the External Quest, the Don Quixote Behaviors, to try to handle your UPS, as we listed above.

The activation, the NEIR mass, will eventually subside back into your subconscious (hours, days, even months later). However, you have done nothing to reduce that NEIR mass and it will continue to activate into your experience whenever there is an appropriate trigger in your life.

There will always be triggers: it is the nature of life that you win some and you lose some. Nobody has the power to control, to always get what they want in life, especially what others do and say.

The problems with this strategy include:

- Externals do not cause your MODs.

- Even if they did, nobody who has ever lived has had enough power to always control others and external events.

- Addictions and compulsions cause damages to your health, finances, and happiness.

- Your efforts to control others will meet with resistance and conflicts.

- Above all: Your NEIRs continue to exist and to activate. The nature of life is that you win some and you lose. As long as your happiness depends on externals you will live MOD after MOD and your MOPs will be fleeting. Do not expect to be much happier than you have been to date.

- -

Path #2 requires the discreation of the NEIR mass. **Every activation is the opportunity to discreate that NEIR mass.** You cannot discreate anything that you are not experiencing. You cannot discreate your NEIR masses when they are in your subconscious; only when you are experiencing them; i.e. when they are activated.

Illustration: The Two Paths in Life

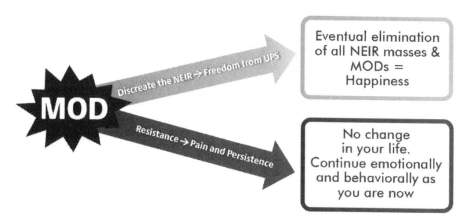

How to Control Your External World

Once you control your internal world, you will discover that you can control your external world to a considerable extent. As you restore your BEing to Essence, your Wisdom, Love, and your Power of manifestation grow. They are, in fact, proportional to your experience and expression of Essence, to your recovery of your Divinity. That recovery starts with the discreation of your counter creations, your suppressions, to your Essence.

Summary:

We repeat the essence of this chapter because this understanding is so critical to your happiness:

**What you do with your activations is
critical to your True Happiness.**

You have TWO PATHS:

#1- The Road of No-action and Continued UPS

If you ignore your MODs, or suppress them, drug them, or plaster over them with MOPs; they will eventually subside back into your subconscious. You will be free experientially of that neg-emo, but only for a while; until the next trigger. That NEIR mass remains within you, latent in your subconsciousness, like a loaded gun ready to fire again when life pulls your trigger. The next trigger will again shoot it into your experience, where you will again suffer that same UPS - over and over and over again until you discreate it. That is the Sisyphean way to happiness: does not work.

> **Illustration: Sisyphus:** In Greek mythology, Sisyphus was the king of what is now Corinth. The gods punished for his hubris and trickery by sentencing him for all eternity to roll an immense boulder up a mountain where, near the top, it would slip out of his grasp and roll back down. He had to start all over. Sisyphean efforts are those that can never bear fruit, no matter how many times attempted.

#2- The Highway to Happiness

The "Highway to Happiness" to take each activation as it occurs (or as soon as possible if you can't process at that moment) and discreate the NEIR. That liberates your neg-emo and frees you of the MOD. Repeat this on every activation and eventually you will be free of all UPS.

In the Psycanics Life Transformation System, students keep a logbook of their activations and negative Causal Sequences. They then systematically process each one. This leads to eventual discreation of all their NEIR masses such that they no longer have any activations.

Again: Apply BTT to every activation and eventually you will have no activations. You will live in serenity and peace, wisdom and power.

19- Finding Your Identities

The interior life of most people is a jungle of ECRE of all kinds about which they have only minimal distinctions and less control. There are positive and negative Essence identities, human roles, characters, personality, the mind with its myriad kinds of thoughts, the emotions, impulses and compulsions to behaviors, addictions, painful memories and traumas, many erroneous beliefs, programs and paradigms, victim, and many other types of energies and aberrations, which we will get to in the advanced books.

In learning psycanics, you are learning internal gardening and re-decoration. Using BTT, you can weed out your negative ECRE and plant positive identities-realities-experience to convert your internal jungle to a garden of Happiness. There is a Hi Road, a direct path, a shortcut, a fast track, to doing this: transform your NEIRs to PEIRS. If you had to discharge-discreate all your negative ECRE one by one, it would take lifetimes. By going directly to the creator (you-the-BEing) and re-creating the creator, all your creations change automatically to conform to your new YOU.

The essence of BTT (Being Transformation Technology) is to:

Find — *in your experience (FEELing), not in your mind (THINKing)*-- your NEIRs and discreate them. Then re-create your Self as PEIRS. This will "magically" change the other elements of that Causal Sequence in your life. Repeat discreation on every NEIR mass, and you will soon transform all your life.

The Causal Sequence of Life starts with **BE→FEEL: your identities determine your emotions**. Your emotions=/-, remember, are your self-love+/-.

- Positive emotions show you that you have activated a PEIR. You are BEing a positive WPVLJ identity and you are loving yourself, which is the foundation of True Happiness.

- Negative emotions tell you that you have activated a NEIR. You are experiencing neg-emo, which is neg-self-love for BEing in an anti-WPVLJ identity (PEIR). TIME TO DISCREATE!

Inside every MOD activation (neg-emo), there is always one or more NEIRs.

Before you can discreate a NEIR, you must find it in your experience, by feeling it. Do not use your mind for this! Fortunately, it is relatively simple to feel inside your neg-emo and find the NEIR in your experience. You then let yourself BE it, which is to FEEL it. It your BEing your NEIR, BE-FEELing it, that discreates it.

Experience versus Mind

You-psycan have two modalities of operation: Experience-feeling and mind-thinking. **ALL DISCREATION TAKES PLACE in EXPERIENCE**. Thinking, being in your mind, attending to your thoughts, blocks discreation because it blocks direct experience of your ECRE. (This is why mental psycho-therapies (such as psychoanalysis) that focus on thinking about, remembering, analyzing, talking about, or trying to understand your problems take so long and, even so, have such poor results. *(I have had more than one student stand up in a seminar and say that he had achieved more change in one BTT session than he had in years of psychotherapy.)* Not only is mind, memory, understanding unnecessary to resolve your problems; it is a great waste of TE (Time and Energy) of the explorer and the pilot. *(I will say more on the FEEL<>THINK dichotomy in Section II of this book.)*

The essence of BTT is you-psycan-creator-consciousness go into your BEing. Your BEing comprises the Shell which includes all your psycanic ECRE generating all your human experience. In BTT, you-Aware-Will go directly to your psycanic reality causing your neg-experience or behavior. You then discreate it. You then create any positive realities you want to experience in the future. Your realities are your creations; they are you ECRE, masses of energy existing **in present time**. Just discreate them. **We don't care why, when, or how you created them – and knowing any of that will not discreate them.** Don't waste BTT on "mind shit".

A Note about Time

The past (time) is an illusion; it does not exist. Nor does the future. Time is an illusion created by the mind, by labels of "past" or "future" on present time realities-experiences. **The only time that ever exists is the present** (in Essentiality, the Eternal Present). What we call the past is you-psycan looking at memories (mental realities) or experiencing emotions created in the "past" which at the time, was the present. Those mental images and emotions are ECRE **existing now, in present time.** You are labeling ("meta-reality-ing") them "the past". (Meta-realities are explained later.)

You-psycan created your pictures and emo "of the past" in some incident which was then the present moment, **and they are still with you.** For example, a traumatic incident from your past is an energy recording during that incident (including a NEIR mass activation), which NEIR mass is still with you. It can be triggered by "memories" which is just looking at your present time mental pictures of the incident. You create the illusion of time by creating and holding a label of "the past" on that piece of your ECRE. However, that **ECRE recording of the incident is existing in your BEing in present time.**

To free yourself of that "past", simply discreate the ECRE, now. You don't need any reference to the past, or where or when or why. All experience is the impact of realities on consciousness: discreate the reality to change the experience; no complications needed.

UHBs firmly believe in the reality and power of past. They drag with them through life a lot of negative "past" ECRE: "history" and "baggage" such as traumatic memories, resentments, guilt, errors and failures, victim of others, they-done-me-wrong; they-owe-me, etc.). UHBs also believe that the past formed them and controls them even in the present; that they can't change many of effects on them of the past.

All this is great for Drama and UPS. And a marvelous hallucination. An SEB has discreated all "past" ECRE. He retains any memories he chooses, but **has zero charge on anything in his "past".** He has discreated all resentment, guilt, victim, traumas, etc. He has forgiven anyone who did give him anti-love, including anything negative he did to himself. He has closed all terminated relationships *energetically* so that he is in appreciation and love for that person and gratitude for the experience. He knows that nobody owes him anything (outside of any signed debt agreements). He knows that influence of the past is minimal compared to his will and power to create his BEing and his present time life as he desires.

All of this discreation and more is necessary for Enlightenment, to lighten your Shell of the human illusion and so recover your perception of your True Being (psycan) and communication with Essence.

Back to THINK versus FEEL

If you are not sure of the (huge) difference between the two modalities of THINK and FEEL, between mind and experience, the Psycanics BTT Course has meditative exercises that guide you to first distinguish you-psycan from your human being, and then to distinguish {**consciousness-feeling-experience**} <> {**mind-thoughts-thinking**}.

You must identify your NEIRs in your experience, by feeling them, not by thinking of them or verbalizing them. Remember, **your NEIRs are not thoughts or beliefs, nor are they the words you use to describe them.** Your NEIRs are masses of subtle, psycanic energy that cause you-consciousness the *experience* of BEing that way. You FEEL that they are who you are, even that they are the truth of who you are.

Identities are subtle experiences compared to your emotions which are grosser forms of energy. However, they are more powerful than emotions. They *CAUSE* emotions. Identities are the experience of BEing that way, not the thought, belief, nor the verbal statement or description of the experience. We will often use "BE-FEEL" to mean integrating with and letting yourself BE and FEEL the experience of you being the NEIR.

You MUST identify your NEIRs in your experience for two reasons:

#1- Your mind will lie to you to protect you from confronting or "suffering" your NEIR. It will present you with thoughts and ideas that are NOT your NEIRs to "save" you from BEing them, because they are UPS and because you have an opinion-creation that it is Bad-SNB to BE a NEIR (later chapter on this).

#2- You cannot discreate in mind, only in experience. Your will is your innate power to create. Your consciousness is your innate power to experience and experience discreates. Only experience discharges the energy from a reality, not THINKing: mind cannot discreate anything. Mind is part of the creation process. You create all your thoughts and can energize the desired ones to manifest including into your FU.

The mind is so powerful in trying to protect you from negative experience, that it is a major problem in BTT, sometimes even with experienced explorers. Ever-present is the tendency of rock (TT) explorers to go off into mind and out of experience (which stops discreation). Both the explorer and the pilot must be always alert to this and immediately return the explorer to experience.

You remember there are five families of neg-emo:

1. **Anger** which includes impatience, frustration, impotence, rage, hate, etc.

2. **Fear** which includes anxiety, worry, uncertainty, shyness, timidity, terror, etc.

3. **Sorrow** which includes sadness, loneliness, melancholy, grief, mourning, etc.

4. **Guilt** which includes embarrassment, shame, regret, remorse, etc.

5. **Depression** which includes dejection, despair, apathy, hopelessness, etc.

It can help to find your NEIRs to know that there is a dependable relationship between your NEIRs and your emotions. These are:

1- **Anger: Present Time Anti-Power**: I am unable, I cannot (do or get whatever), I am incapable.

2- **Fear: Future Time Anti-Power:** I am <u>not going to be able</u> to (do, avoid, stop, whatever).

3- **Sadness, sorrow:** A- **Anti-value**: I am not good enough; I am less than; I am unworthy, undeserving, nobody loves me, etc.

                    B- **Past Time Anti-Power**: I could not do it; I am a failure.

4- **Guilt: Anti-Love:** I am bad (bad person, bad daughter, bad parent, etc.) (because I did something bad/wrong).

5- **Depression**: Forever Time Anti-Power. "I can't do it and <u>I will never be able</u> to." (Helplessness + Hopelessness).

Too simple, right?

Many times, you will be able to will to open up to your neg-emo and directly feel your NEIR. If not, here are examples of the questions that pilots use to help the explorer find his NEIR.

> **Anger**: Present Time Anti-Power: Exactly what are you angry about? What is it you cannot do or get in that situation? The response, "I <u>can't</u> get (*whatever -- for example, my spouse to listen, or my children to obey*) is the verbalization of his experience of the NEIR. The NEIR is the <u>experience</u> of not having power, of not being able to (whatever).

> **Fear**: Future Time Anti-Power: Exactly what are you afraid of? What is the bad thing that could happen that you are not going to be able to handle: avoid, stop, remedy, etc.? The <u>experience</u> of "I am not going to be able" is the NEIR.

> **Sorrow**: Sadness is usually anti-value (A), but can sometimes be fixed, past, anti-power, i.e. failure (B)

A- **Anti-value**: The exact flow of questions to find the NEIR behind sadness varies depending on what the trigger event is, but the flow always starts with: Exactly what is so sad? How do you feel about yourself; who are you in relation to that event? How did they treat you? Who are you that people treat you that way?

Examples:

I was not invited to the party. What kind of people are not invited to parties? Who/how are you that people don't invite you to parties? Answer examples: I am less than others. I am not good enough. Nobody loves me.

Loneliness: Why do people leave you alone? Who are you that people don't care about you; don't want to be with you? How are you that nobody loves you?

Sadness, sorrow, grief: A- *My child died / My dog died*. How do you feel and who are you without your dog? Example answer: *alone, unloved*. Who are you that people don't love you? NEIRs: **I am not good enough; I am less than the others; I am unworthy, undeserving.**

B- Sadness from Past Time Anti-Power: The explorer will report an error or failure of some kind. The NEIR is the experience of anti-power: **I could not do it; or I am a failure. I am not good enough.**

> **Guilt**: The NEIR is always some form of "I am bad". To take an explorer into the experience: What did you do wrong? *(Explorer answers with whatever.)* What kind of person does that? *Bad people.* Given that you did that, who are you and how does it feel to be a bad person (or whatever the failed role is)? The experience of being bad is the NEIR.

> **Depression**: Forever Time Anti-Power. Exactly what are you depressed about; what is it that you can't do and feel you will never be able to? When the explorer answers with what is that they are depressed about, send them into their experience of anti-power and hopelessness. The energy of "I will never be able to" (whatever) is the NEIR.

Should you have any trouble finding your NEIRs behind any neg-emo or any neg-behavior (relationship problems, addictions, traumas, whatever), you will find expert pilots to guide you in the online support groups.

Bad to be Bad

When piloting, either yourself or others: Be careful to never confuse the identity of "Bad" with the opinion of "Bad-SNB". **When dealing with any NEIR, there will be an opinion of Bad-SNB** to the NEIR. Therefore, with the NEIR of "I am bad", **there will be an opinion that "it is bad to be bad".** Y

I am a bad person (bad father/mother, bad son/daughter, bad salesperson, bad whatever role in life) is an identity.

To the bad role/identity, the explorer will have created an opinion of Bad-SNB: eg: "It is bad to be a bad father"; "It is bad to be a bad daughter", etc.

You must first discreate the opinion that it is bad to be bad before discreating the identity of "I am bad". *(More on this in the Discreation section, in the chapters on resistance and the Hallucination of Bad-SNB.)"*

Exercise

Use this form to practice finding your NEIRs. See if you can find your NEIR in 10 MODs (10 different activations of your neg-emotions.) *You will find more sophisticated forms and the MOD logbook in the BTT Course*

The Three Columns:

1. **Trigger event:** whatever situation is setting off your MOD activation.

2. **Neg-Emo:** Put the family: anger, fear, sadness, guilt, depression.

3. **NEIR:** It will be anti-WPVLJ: wisdom, power, value, goodness/love.

	My Trigger Event	My Neg-Emo	My NEIR(s)
1			
2			
3			
4			
5			
6			
7			
8			
9			
10			

Once you have identified in experience your NEIRs, the next step is to discreate them. This Book I introduces how to discreate. The complete information on discreation is the subject of Book II.

20- The Discreation Protocol

This chapter presents the basic, 15-step procedure for discreating NEIRs and re-creating your Self in PEIRs. A pilot will vary it depending on the needs of the explorer, but you will have to follow it exactly. The BTT Course includes recordings which guide you through these steps. The recordings allow you, the explorer, to stay focused on your experience and discreation without out having to read the steps and so go into minds. (Note: There are more complicated protocols in the advanced levels of BTT that produce quicker and deeper results, but all your learning starts with these.)

1. Trigger your MOD if you are not already activated: Put yourself in the trigger situation or imagine it so you activate in the negative emotion. Open to feeling your neg-emo. Note what the emotion is and remember the table of correspondence of emotions to NEIRs if you need help find the NEIR.

2. Emotions: Penetrate your neg-emo and find and feel -- in your experience, not in mind – your NEIR. If you find more than one NEIR, take the leftmost in the sequence of Wisdom→Power→Value→Bad.

   ➢ If you are a rock (Book II), do not worry about the NEIR until your feeling is restored. **Stay in your neg-emotions** until you have rehabilitated your openness to feel, until you can feel your neg-emo easily and comfortable. **This may take multiple sessions.** There are also protocols to open rocks, for example, by discreating fear of suffering.

> ➢ If you are jello (Book II), **you need control**. You must control your attention, not go to Victim and "poor me", not suffer, and **not get lost** in your charges. Go through the emotion as quickly as possible to your resistance to the NEIR. (Neg-emo is proportional to the Rxx).

3. Resistance: discreate: Open your feeling to experience, to BE-FEEL, your NEIR. Feel for any resistances to BEing your NEIR. Rule: **Your neg-emo is result of and proportional to your resistance to the NEIR**. Ergo, if you have neg-emo, you are resisting the NEIR.

4. Discreate the resistance to our NEIR:

   a. Discreate the Opinion of Bad-SNB to the NEIR.

   b. If you can't do that, discreate the resistance itself with Exp2.

   Once the resistance is discharged sufficiently that it will not interfere with you experiencing your NEIR, proceed to next step. (You do not have to discreate the resistance or neg-emo completely, only reduce so you can easily feel your NEIR.)

5. **Discreate NEIR: Integrate** with NEIR and BE your NEIR. Surrender to BEing the NEIR. Feel it, experience it, BE-FEEL it. Remember not to take it seriously; it is merely ECRE and therefore an illusion; not the Truth of who you are. Stay in the NEIR until the experience is minimal or completely gone. Focus again on the trigger whenever you need help to activate more NEIR.

6. Optional: Use CCC (Creation-Counter-Creation, explained later) to activate even more NEIR and to transition to and energize the PEIR. (You will need the PEIR from the next step for this.)

7. **Decide your PEIR**: who you are going to BE instead of the NEIR? This should include the polar opposite of your NEIR and you can add in other identities as desired. Create (mockup in imagination), or go to the past and bring to the present, the reality-*experience of BEing* that PEIR.

8. **Energize, Real-ize, your PEIR**: Once you have the identity real, fiat it (decide to BE it), and with your divine creator will, energize that experience. Intention it, enjoy it, love it, wallow in it. The more you energize the identity, the more massive and permanent it will be. You are using the same power with which you created the NEIR now to create the PEIR. Note how real you made your negative BE-FEEL, your MODs -- you have the same power to create PEIRs and self-love.

9. **FEEL**: Your PEIR will naturally activate positive self-love emotions. Energize them even more. Decide that you will BE-FEEL that way all the time, and especially in that trigger event.

10. **THINK**: With your PEIR activated: Check your THINK, your mental realities, for any negative or limiting beliefs and programs that you created at the effect of your NEIR. Discreate with Exp2 and change them to positive realities. (This is explained in Book III.)

11. **DO and RELATE:** With your PEIR activated, visualize your new, desired, positive DO: Energize how are you going to behave, act, or perform when that trigger occurs. Re-live in your imagination your new DO or RELATEing and program and energize your new behaviors.

12. **HAVE**: Likewise: create, imagine, energize and enjoy mentally your new, desired results. Live the experience of already HAVE-ing them. As a result, in the change in who you are (PEIRs), how you feel (positive emotions), your change of THINK and of DO, you will naturally have different results in your life. Energize these.

13. **Immediate Verification:** Once you have your positive Causal Sequence created and energized to your satisfaction, imagine yourself in the trigger event again, and any other situation that activated your NEIR. If anything activates, discreate it repeating this protocol.

14. **Final Verification:** The ultimate test is always your change of experience when confronting the trigger event in real life. If the trigger event occurs again and you still activate, you have a deeper level of the NEIR mass available for discreation. Repeat the protocol.

15. Finally: celebrate your power over your experience and your liberty. Once you can control your psycanic experience, you are free of the world. The world can no longer (appear) to cause your UPS, and you know that it has no power to produce your Happiness: everything is in your hands.

21- The 7 Conditions

**The Cycle of Existence of all realities has three phases:
Creation→Experience→Discreation.**

**The purpose of a creation is experience.
A creation persists until it fulfills its purpose.**

There are 7 Conditions the explorer must fulfill for to discreation to occur. Where any condition is deficient, discreation will either be slow, painful, or not take place at all. Thus, we can also call them the 7 Discreation Stoppers.

The 7 Conditions for Discreation, which when not fulfilled, become the 7 Discreation Stoppers, are:

1- Responsable Creator. No Victim.

2- Commitment to Results and to avoid Drama.

3- Stay in Experience and out of mind.

4- Rocks<>Jellos: Know what kind of explorer you are and follow the relevant protocol. Rocks: stay in emotions to rehabilitee FEEL. Jellos: maintain consciousness and control.

5- Discreate Resistance, by Exp2, or by discreation of Hallucination of Bad-SNB.

6- Discreate any meta-realities.

7- Do not get caught in the meta-reality of "truth", if so discreate.

The 7 Conditions in more detail:

1- The explorer must BE in the identity of Creator and taking Responsibility for his ECRE. He cannot be in Victim or blaming others for his experience. You must exit the Fatal Identity Sequence, Victim, and Drama by acknowledging you are Cause-Creator of your RExp.

2- The explorer must understand Drama versus Results, and decide that he wants Results (easy, fast discreation) instead of Drama (long BTT sessions in Victim with poor results and "fireworks" (lots of neg-emo)).

3- The explorer must stay in experience, in FEEL; and out of mind, of THINKing (analysis, understanding, observing, remembering, etc.).

4- Jello explorers must move from Victim-Effect of their experience to Cause and take control of their attention and energies. No Drama! Avoid getting lost in charges.

   Rock explorers must rehabilitate their power to feel and become a jello without losing their cause and control. They must learn to stay out of mind and in experience.

5- The explorer must discreate enough Resistance to any RExp that it does not interfere with his experience of that RExp. Become Space to your creations.

6- The explorer or his pilot must recognize and discreate any meta-realities before discreating the main RExp.

7- The explorer must understand the difference between truth and reality. If any RExp appears to be truth, to discreate that experience as a meta-reality. Never believe in your NEIRs or take them seriously.

Resistance to Feeling or to the NEIR

Of the 7 Conditions, the one that causes the most problems in BTT is Resistance.

Law: The Three Phases of the Cycle of Existence of a creation are:

Creation=Reality→Experience→Discreation

**All resistance to (the experience of) a reality sticks
the Cycle of Existence in the phase 2, in "Experience"
so that the reality does not proceed to Discreation.**

Resistance (Rxx), both in the electrical circuits and in psycanic discreation, reduces or completely stops the flow of energy. Rxx (Resistance) in Psycanics is the negation to experience which obviously will stick the Cycle of Discreation in **experience and so stop discreation.**

**Neg-emo is directly proportional to the
creation of Bad-SNB→Rxx to the NEIR.**

**To the degree the explorer is in neg-emo, he is resisting the NEIR.
Discreate the Rxx before trying to discreate the NEIR.**

**Beginning explorers spend more time discreating Rxx
than they spend discreating the NEIRs themselves.**

Having to discreate resistance can extend a BTT session from 40 minutes to 1.5 hours, and even to requiring several sessions. **Resistance also turns the negative experience of the NEIR into suffering by persisting and extending the neg-emo.**

Practiced explorers have transcended all creation of resistance by transcending their hallucination of Bad-SNB. They do not create Bad-SNB to anything. They can, therefore, enter directly into the NEIR and can usually discreate it in as little as 40 minutes total session time.

We will cover all of the 7 Conditions in depth in Book II. They are not only critical to easy and quick discreation, they are major principles by which to operate your life and are essential to True Happiness.

22- Your Creation of PEIRs

In BTT, it is essential to balance your TE (Time and Energy) to negatives with equal or more TE to positives. Excessive focus on negatives will eventually energize and therefore reinforce the negatives instead of discreating them. Your attention (TE) is energy and energy energize realities. In fact, eventually, after about 100 of Basic BTT, **all explorers must advance to Accelerated BTT because Basic BTT begins to reinforce negatives (NEIRs)** too much. Accelerated BTT is just that: quick and universal discreation of NEIR masses.

Technically, you do not have to create PEIRs; you are Essence and your spiritual nature includes the four PEIRs: WPVLJ. They are currently suppressed by your NEIRs (and other, deeper creations discussed in Essentiality). However, it is productive to balance negative and positive energy, and to energize your PEIRs to grow their mass and reality, which is creation. So, we will hold to the idea that you must create your PEIRs.

Key Concepts

Creation is to Cause something new to exist, something that did not exist before the creative act. You create art, your relationships, your family and children, a business, a new product, etc.

Manifestation is to Cause to enter your experience, to pull or attract into your life, something already created by others. You manifest a spouse, money, a car, a house, a job, etc. as these have been created by others.

The **willful energization** procedure for both creation and manifestation is the same and we will use the words interchangeably with either including the other.

Fiat (TT): A fiat is an **act of your will**, your creative decision, that a reality BE, that it come into existence. The word is taken from the Christian Bible in Latin, in Genesis, where God is creating the universe and She starts with "FIAT LUX": Let There Be Light. As a "chip off the old block" of Essence, a child of Essence, you have innately this Power of Creation. You have your Essence, your spirituality, well suppressed so you can BE human and powerless to maintain Game Conditions and Drama.

Energy: the fundamental substance of all the exists. Everything that exists is formed of energy. Essence radiates energy and out of that energy, Her own Substance, all realities, the entire Creation, is formed. Your power of creation is to take energy and form it into realities, particularly your psycanics realities. You can also manifest into your physical experience your desired realities by energizing the psycanic reality model of what you want. Again, this power is counter-created by your NEIRs so that manifestation in the FU is difficult, iffy and retarded to maintain Game Conditions and Drama.

Creation is the reverse of discreation. Creation and manifestation are a matter of using your will and power of imagination / visualization to create a **mockup**, an initial, psycanic reality-experience of your desired new RExp, and then **using your will to direct energy into that reality** until it has sufficient mass to persist and now determine your experience.

Realities: Realities are masses of modulated energy, energy taking on an identity to be something in particular. All realities are creations; someone, somewhere, sometime had to create them. Nothing springs into existence without a Cause. For everything your experience, you-spirit are that cause; you-psycan are the creator.

Discreation is a matter of using your will to focus on the undesired reality-experience and opening your consciousness (power of perception and feeling) to experience that reality until you have discharged all the energy from it. The basic law is Experience Experienced Disappears (Exp2$\rightarrow$0).

Blocks to Manifestation

Right now, as an ordinary human being, you have a lot of subconscious realities against this manifestation working easily and quickly for you, both for your PU and your FU. This helps you to maintain Game Conditions and Drama. We will take up those counter-realities in Book III when we get to your HAVE and how to manifest in your FU.

Essentiality contains knowledge to advance for the understanding and/or acceptance of ordinary, unenlightened human beings. One example of this is the full information about creation. For example, just the statement: "**You are the creator of everything in your lif**e" will seem unreal, even ridiculous, to UHBs. And that is the low gradient. The full truth is: "**You are the creator of the physical universe and everything in it**". Your power over the FU is proportional to your transcension of the Human Illusion and Return to Essence. An example of this is Jesus who achieved his re-integration with the One and therefore instant and total Power over the FU, over his own Essence.

That you are the creator of your FU is far beyond the reality horizon of most human beings; it will seem preposterous. However, if you study Essentiality, you will come to see why and how it is true. In this book, we have started with the lowest gradient of awakening your Creator Within, showing you how you are the creator of your identities, neg-emo, NEIR masses, your hallucinations of Bad-SNB, and therefore of your happiness<>UPS. Until this book, you have been living in the Fatal Identity Sequence hallucinating that external things cause your psycanic experience. You are also hallucinating that you have no power over the FU, a creation necessary to Game Conditions and Drama, the purposes of your Human Incarnation.

In Book III of this BTT Self Therapy series, we will go into the second part of the Causal Sequence of Life: THINK, DO, HAVE. We will show you how you are creating Drama instead of Results in those Arenas of your life. In this chapter, we are addressing only your creation of PEIRs which will then generate positive FEEL, and requires a little addition creation of your desired result in each area: positive THINK, DO, HAVE.

Creating PEIRs

The first step is to discreate your NEIRs. The Law of Creation is:

**You cannot create positive over the top of negative;
you must first discreate the negatives to create Space, ergo
absence of counter- realities to the positive.**

There are three reasons for this Law:

1- Your subconscious is full of negatives, of NEIR masses. Like an old house full of decrepit furniture, you have little room, no Space, for new furniture. New furniture would just get lost in all the old and not make much difference to your experience of living in the house. You must first "clean house": discreate your NEIRs to make Space for your PEIRs.

2- To overcome NEIRs with only the creation of positives (PEIRs), you would need many times the amount of energization that you do if there were no NEIRs to over-create.

3- If you don't discreate your NEIR masses, they will remain in your subconsciousness forever* and always be subject to activation by any trigger. When triggered, they will overwrite your experience of your PEIRs (as they do now, which is why MOPs are fleeting) and you will be back in their UPS - over and over again.

Essentiality: When we say forever here, we mean *forever*, because you-psycan drag your NEIR masses with you from incarnation to incarnation. A Human Adventure Exploration Cycle is from 500 to 700 incarnations. You-psycan explore as much as of human experience as you can: you have been male◇ female, straight◇gay, black◇white, rich◇poor, saint◇sinner, priest◇prostitute, soldier◇merchant, healthy◇sickly, strong◇weak, king◇beggar, smart◇stupid, etc. You have died tortured, buried alive, crucified, burned, drowned, crushed, imprisoned, and occasionally of old age in your bed. In the advanced forms of BTT in Essentiality, should you go so far, you will process any negative energy you are carrying from your past lives. Otherwise, past lives have little importance in your spiritual development. (I have processed hundreds of past lives, my own and those of others. At one time, for about 2 years in my 40 years of investigation, I thought they were important and did lots of regressions.)

Your HIC (Human Identity Complex), like your body, dissipates after each incarnation, and you manifest a new one for your next lifetime. However, your NEIR masses are not human; they are spiritual creations and you carry them in your Shell from life to life until you discreate them. You will not be able to leave Samsara (your cycle of human incarnations on Earth) until you have discreated them. All this is explained in Essentiality where you will experience these things for yourself.

- -

C C C = Creation Counter-Creation, and
I C I = Intention Counter-Intention.

It is one of the Laws of Creation that:

CCC: The effort to create a positive reality will activate negative realities already present in your BEing.

ICI: The Intention to DO anything will activate any blocks and counter-intentions to that action already present in your BEing.

CCC and ICI are very useful for bringing into your consciousness the negative realities that you need to discreate so that the positive manifests easily in the Space that you have opened by discreating the negatives. The training of how to do this is in the Psycanics' BTT Course. However, it is so simple that you may be able to experience it here and now. Just follow these instructions:

Close your eyes and relax.

1.   Clear your mind of thoughts.

2.   Mockup and fiat (willfully create) the reality-identity-experience: "I am the powerful creator of my life."

3.   Energize that identity until the counter-identities or neg-emotions activate into your experience.

4.   Check your experience: Is it real that you are a powerful creator of your life, or do you feel some other, some negative experience? Your negative experiences here are your counter-RExps (Reality→Experience) to the positive identity you are wanting to create.

5.   In a full BTT process (as opposed to this example of simply identifying your counter RExp), you would then alternate between discreation of negative and creation of positive. You would discharge your negative identity of Not-creator, and then go back to energizing your positive reality desired (#3). You would repeat this process until you have de-energized your negative RExp (it ceases to exist) and energized the positive (I am Powerful) so that it is massive and real all the time. You have thus transformed your RExp. You will have transformed your BEing from that NEIR to the PEIR.

Examples of NEIRs that could appear in this CCC include: I am not powerful, I am not creator, I can't do it; I am a failure. These are what you would discreate.

It is also possible that you will get neg-emo instead of NEIRs: frustration, anger, sadness, depression, etc. In this case, you need to penetrate the emotion to find the NEIR as shown in the chapter: How To Find Your NEIRs.

In BTT, it is very important to balance negative with positive. An explorer just beginning to learn BTT, will spend more time discreating negatives than energizing positives. As he advances, more and more TE will be given to the positive. In the fourth level of BTT, BTT Accelerated, the discreation of negatives is very fast and 75% of the TE is in positive, in the energization of PEIRs.

If any of this seems confusing or complicated, we recommend you take the Psycanics BTT course and then join a support group where you will have professional pilots guiding you step-by-step to learn everything in the three books of this series.

23- What Now?

The question is: Do you want all that you have studied to remain in mere theory, or do you want to apply it and make changes in your life? Remember those changes can range from:

➤ just eliminating one **Trigger→NEIR→Neg-emo** sequence; to

➤ eliminating all your most painful MODs; to

➤ elimination an addiction or phobia or block to action, to

➤ cleaning up an entire Arena (such as your relationships) to

➤ achieving True Happiness by eliminating all your NEIR masses.

No matter what depth of work on yourself you choose, it requires you to take action. You have to learn BTT and then practice it until you achieve your desired results. (We recommend an hour per day.) Remember the difference between study and learning: studying is understanding; learning is able to apply and produce the desired results. No results, no learning. People can study a lot and learn little.

The next steps in the Psycanics' Life Transformation System are:

1- **Read Book II** - contents explained below.

2- **Take the BTT Course** (after Book III or concurrently). This comprises guided processes to assure that you experience BTT and all the relevant phenomena: will, consciousness, experience versus mind, realities, how to discreate the Fatal Identity, the Hallucination of Bad-SNB, and the creation of PEIRs.

3- Weekly **Online Pilot Support, Level 1.** You make a list of the negative situations in your life that you want to eliminate in the order you want to eliminate them. Attend the online support sessions where you will be guided by professional pilots to your desired results. After a few weeks of this, you will see the results in your life. This first level support group deals with BE, FEEL, and Resistance: you learn to handle emotions, resistance to feeling and to NEIRs, how to discreate NEIRs and create PEIRs. You will be learning to pilot yourself, and you can always come back to the online sessions when you need help.

4- **Read Book III** which deals with the other Arenas of the Causal Sequence: THINK, RELATE, DO, and HAVE. This book gives you all the theory of how to trace any negative experience in these Arenas (for example, addictions and relationship problems) back to the Causal NEIR. (You already know how to discreate NEIRs and have available the online support sessions for any difficulties.)

5- **Weekly Online Pilot Support, Level 2.** In these sessions, you choose what you want to transform in the THINK, RELATE, DO, and HAVE Arenas: Relationships, health, eliminate addictions, phobias, block to action, fear, traumatic incidents, PTSD: whatever you wish in the order you wish. The pilot both guides you and teaches how to achieve your desired results.

6- **There are more levels beyond these.** For example, in one level, you learn Accelerated BTT and how to discreate your NEIR masses "wholesale". In another, you clean your BEing of all negative energy: of the past, your childhood, all painful and embarrassing incidents, guilt, and you close energetically all past relationships. We need not concern ourselves with these now.

BOOK II

Book II presents all the 7 Conditions for Creation and Discreation in detail. The mechanisms behind the 7 Conditions are also fundamental factors in all human experience and behavior. Not-knowing these elements of existence keep the UHB in Game Conditions and Drama. They are the mechanisms of most relationship problems and conflicts (a favorite Arena for Drama).

On understanding all in this book, you will experience a new level of awareness of how life really works, some degree of awakening from the Human Dream.

The contents of Book II include:

➤ The 7 Conditions for Creation and Discreation

➤ The Fatal Identity Sequence: the Great Hallucination in which the human being live that kills his creator power and keeps him in Game Conditions → poor results → Drama and UPS.

➤ The Fatal Identity

➤ The Fatal Paradigm

➤ Victim

➤ External Quest

➤ The Merry-Go-Round

➤ The Don Quixote Syndrome.

➤ Responsability and Power

➤ Feel versus Think: Experience versus Mind

➤ Rocks and Jellos

➤ Meta-Realities

➤ Truth versus Reality, and Mu

➤ Resistance

➤ The Hallucination of Bad-SNB.

➤ The 12 Great Hallucinations of the Human Being.

The Levels of BTT:

BTT has multiple skill and power levels. By skill, we mean that the explorer grows his comprehension and his ability to handle energy to create and discreate. By power, we mean that as your skill grows, you will be able to discreate bigger and bigger realities faster and faster.

Level 1- Exp2: Experienced Experience Disappears.

In this level, you learn to apply everything in this book. _**Study**_ is to **understand** information intellectually (if there is no understanding, the study TE has achieve nothing). Study must not be confused with _**learning**_ which is the ability to apply, to DO, and produce the desired results.

If you do not achieve your desired results, you have not learned no matter how much you have studied. It is quite common that people study a lot and learn little.

In this level, which includes this book, the **Psycanics BTT Course, Level 1**; and the **Level 1 Support Groups**; you learn:

- The basics of PECRED: Psycan, Energy, Creation, Reality, Experience, Discreation.

- Distinguish you-psycan, your spiritual BEing of Aware-Will, from you-human and from your mind.

- Transcend the Fatal Identity and its Fatal Sequence.

- Take Responsability for your Experience (Resp Exp) and exit Victim.

- To eschew Drama, the human default for experience, and commit to Results.

- Differentiate between FEELing and THINKing. Discreation occurs _**only**_ in FEELing, never in mind: THINKing stops discreation.

- To discreate resistance (Rxx) to your negative RExp.

- To identify your hallucinations of Bad-SNB that trigger your Rxx.

- To discreate your creations-realities of Bad-SNB.

- To recognize meta-realities that interfere with discreation.

- To distinguish between realities and truth; your NEIR are never truth.

- Penetrate your neg-emo to find your NEIRs.

- Discreate your NEIRs with Exp2.

- Re-Create your Self in PEIRs.

- As regards the Causal Sequence, you are learning only FEEL→BE, which is fundamental to Level 2. Book 2 and Level 2 deal with the second part of the Causal Sequence: THINK, RELATE, DO, and HAVE.

Level 2 - CDT = Creation and Discreation Technology.

Book III is the textbook for this level. You learn to fill in your Causal Sequence charts starting from any Arena: to take ANY negative in ANY of the other 4 Arenas of your life (THINK, DO, RELATE, HAVE), and trace it back to the **causal NEIR** for discreation.

You then re-create your BEing in PEIRs and then **create your desired positive experience in all the other arenas of that Causal Sequence**. Level 2 expands your knowledge and skills beyond only FEEL→BE to: **Any Arena→BE**.

In Level 2, you learn how to handle your:

Negative THINK

Your negative THINK includes many neg-energy thought forms: invalidations, aversions, judgments and criticism, determinations, paradigms, and programs. All these contribute to cause problems and conflicts in your relationships. They are all neg-love; they are UPS for you who creates them, and for others you use them against. Others will resist your neg-love with their own neg-love (e.g. react with anger, resistance, sabotage, etc.). True Spiritual Love is free of ALL negative thoughts and neg-energies about others and events. An SEB is Space and Transparency to others and the world.

Negative DO

Your negative DO also have various sides to it:

A- What are you DOing that you want to stop DOing and can't?

You will learn how to discreate your compulsions to DO things that you know are against your greater good. Examples include addictions to substances (e.g. alcohol, tobacco, etc.) and to excess in activities (e.g. gambling, social media, YouTube, "retail therapy", etc.), and all other compulsions and obsessions.

B- What are you NOT-DOing that you want to or know you should DO?

You will also learn how to discreate all **blocks to positive actions** such as phobias, irresponsibility, laziness, PTSD, writer's block, stage fright, shyness and ability to approach the opposite sex, end a relationship, marry, divorce, change jobs, start a business, etc.

Negative RELATE

Your neg-RELATE is everything you DO in relationships that produce negative reactions in others. If you have any problems in your relationships, you can be sure you have neg-RELATE. It is DOR (Denial of Responsability) and Victim to blame the other person for any neg-energy in your relationships.

In Level 2, you will learn to identify and discreate the primary mechanism that causes the great majority of problems and conflicts in relationships. This will start you on the road to harmony, love and cooperation in all your relationships, all the time. However, the area of RELATE is so big that it requires its own book and level. Good relationships require good communication, which is a book and level of study unto itself.

Negative HAVE

Your Negative Have has two sides:

#1- Positive HAVE: What you want to HAVE that you do not HAVE and therefore want to manifest.

#2- Negative HAVE: what you HAVE and don't want, but have not been able to eliminate: disliked job, debts, health problems, bad relationships, etc.

You will learn how your psycanic creation-realities affect, even completely block, your innate spiritual power to manifest what you want in the physical universe (examples: a new job, a business, success (however you define it), money, a house, a family, etc.) You will learn how to use your innate creator power to energize and attract into your life the physical realities that you wish to experience.

Body and Health: You will learn how your negative emotions that you have repressed into your body cause some of your health problems and how to liberate those energies from your body and organs to heal them.

Level 3: ABTT: Advanced Being Transformation Technology.

You-psycan, the spiritual BEing that you are, have the ability to move in time. (Time itself is an illusion.) Level 3 of BTT deals with very precise piloting of BTT producing fast discreation of NEIR masses. It includes returning in time to the moment that you created them. Discreation in the moment of creation is the most effective technique as **it discreates all the posterior activations of that NEIR mass.** The explorer learns to discreate entire chains of MODs, instead of one-by one.

The next levels belong to Essentiality rather than Psycanics.

Level 4: BTTA: Accelerated BTT.

At this level of Power, you are no longer trying to eliminate a particular negative experience but to clean your entire BEing of all negatives. At this level of Power, you the explorer, no longer discreate NEIR activations one by one, trigger by trigger, or even area by area. **You directly discreate the entire NEIR masses,** without attention to triggers, MODs or even areas of your life.

You have only four (4) NEIR masses, anti-WPVLJ: anti-wisdom, anti-power, anti-value, and anti-love (being bad). In BTTA, you have transcended all creation of Bad-SNB and therefore all resistance. You can then integrate into one of the 4 NEIR masses directly and liberate its energy and then go to PEIR Creation. With this technique, **you do not need to discreate the entire mass! using BTTA, it will begin a process of dissipation by itself.**

This greatly accelerates discreation! It will save you thousands of hours of TE compared to discreating MODs one-by-one. With BTTA, you can discreate all your NEIR masses permanently with about 200 hours of BTTA depending on the quality of the piloting and the exploring.

It is important to mention here that an explorer must eventually progress from BBTT to BTTA because, at a certain point, so much attention to the NEIRs stops discreating them and begins to energize them. A good pilot will recognize when an explorer has reached that point and tell them so.

Level 5 and above: The Essentiality Liberation Technology

Psycanics deals with your "human being", with your human experience and behaviors. Essentiality deals with you as an immortal spiritual being; and with your spiritual relationship to Essence.

Psycan and Essence are not real for most humans; they require Essentiality processes to make them perceptible. Level 5 and above of processing are the province of ELT (Essentiality Liberation Technology). The purpose of these levels is to discreate the Shell, the "electron cloud" (analogy) of realities around you-psycan that act upon you-consciousness to generate your (illusory) experience of being only a human being. The Essentiality School of Accelerated Enlightenment teaches all this. These levels of work on your Self are purely Essentiality and require knowledge beyond Psycanics to understand.

24- Book III

Book I present how the left half of the Causal Sequence works:

BE→FEEL = Identities and Emotions.

Book II presents information critical to both your quality of life and to discreation.

Book III presents how the right half of the Causal Sequence works:

THINK → RELATE & DO → HAVE

In Book III, you will learn how to take any negative experience or undesired behavior in the Arenas of THINK, DO, RELATE, HAVE, and find the causal NEIRs. From the BTT Course and the Online Support Level 1, you already know how to discreate NEIRs re-create your Self, your BEing, in PEIRs. Changing your BEing will change the other Arenas of THINK, RELATE, DO, and HAVE to change with merely visualizing the desired result in each Arena.

Here is a preview of Book III:

THINK

Your mind is your best friend or your worst enemy, depending on whether you understand and control it, or it controls you. You will also learn to recognize all the negative THINK you already are creating and experiencing it without realizing what is going on. Much of all human thought is negative, but we are so used to it, we do not realize what is happening and how much it is consuming our energy and our happiness.

Negative THINK includes: pessimism, superiority and inferiority complexes (which always activate resistance in others), hallucination of Bad-SNB, all other invalidations, dislikes and aversions to others, judgments and criticism, distortion of the facts and of the past, programs about how others or the world should be, and false beliefs, values, and paradigms; to name a few.

We will examine how your mind contributes to your problems, conflicts, and Drama in life, especially in your relationships. We will also see how it either blocks or contributes to your power to manifest what you want in life.

For example: Your dislike of others is ALWAYS because they trigger your dislike of something similar in your Self, which will always be related to a NEIR. When you discreate such NEIRs, your aversion to others disappears.

RELATE: your DO in your Relationships: Say, Treat, Respond.

Your RELATE, you will remember, is all your **DO (actions and behaviors) in relationships:**

A- **Say**: what you say and how you say it. This includes your wisdom and the love<>anti-love with which you communicate.

B- **Act, Behave, Treat, Deal with**: This includes all your actions and behaviors with others, how you treat them: with Responsability, Wisdom, Power, Space, and Love, or with their opposites. If you have problems and conflicts in your relationships, you can be certain that you are using anti-love with them.

C- **Respond** or **React**: how you either **react activated in NEIRs** and using neg-love; or **respond** with wisdom and love to how others treat you, especially when they treat you with anti-love. Are you **reactive** or **creative** in your relationships, cause or effect, creator or victim?

In Book III, you will see your NEIRs are the root cause of almost all your problems and conflicts in relationships. You will learn how to penetrate any conflict in a relationship to find and discreate your NEIRS producing your conflicts. You will see your relationships magically transform from negative energy to positive energy.

Remember, you are 100% responsable for your relationships, not the other person. I know this is a high gradient for most people. UHBs usually live in 0% Responsability: in victim, complaining, blaming, guilting, attacking the other person with negative energy, and trying to change or control the other person: Drama. As the other person will usually resist neg-love, this fills the relationship with each person generating negative energy against the other. The relationship spirals down in a tailspin of neg-love.

In the Fatal Identity Sequence, it always looks like the other person is at fault for almost everything. It is inconceivable to some people they have any Responsability at all for the quality of their relationships! -- a very low level of consciousness.

If you want **power→results→harmony and love** in your relationships, **you must operate in 100% Responsability.** If you don't have the results you want in the relationship; it is up to you to vary your communication and behaviors until you get those results. However, never to the point of selling out your own Self and happiness. If maintaining a relationship requires you to sell out your own happiness, the relationship is way too expensive. End it lovingly and move on.

If you don't feel or believe you are 100% responsable (for anything in your life), you can discreate that reality-experience just like any other. All realities are illusions! The entire Creation is an illusion! The only TRUTH is Essence. Everything else is a created reality, and is subject to discreation, including the physical universe itself (which statement requires Essentiality to understand.).

The root cause of problems and conflicts in relationships is the attempt to negate your NEIRs and BE PEIRs by trying to mold the other person in your image of how s/he should BE.

You want to achieve your experience of BEing PEIRs by changing the other person (who will usually resist your tyranny).

The Great Error of Relationships is your effort to create the other person in your image of how she should BE, instead of re-creating your Self in how you should BE.

Furthermore, you usually try to do this with anti-love, which will be resisted. We all try to preserve our self-determination and liberty.

Discreate your NEIRs and the problems disappear. (It's magical!)

DO: Actions and Behaviors

People have two main kinds of negative behaviors (outside of relationships):

#1- The compulsive DO behaviors such as addictions to substances and addictions to activities. These are where you feel compelled to use substances you know are not in your best interest.

Common substance addictions include alcohol, smoking, tranquilizers, marijuana, and all illegal drugs such as amphetamines, cocaine, opioid, sugar, coca cola and junk food.

Common addictions to distractor activities include over eating, excessive social media, TV, video and computer games, excessive porn or sex, shopping, gambling, excessive cell phone use (caused by loneliness or fear of something happening to loved ones.

Behind all additions are NEIRs. In Book 3, you will learn how to take any addiction, to a substance or to an activity, and free yourself of it with BTT.

Law:

The power of your addiction over you is the power of your unconscious will to avoid experiencing your NEIR masses.

Track your neg-DO back to the neg-FEEL you are avoiding and you will find the NEIR.

**Discreate the NEIR and the addiction disappears.
More magic!**

#2- The compulsive NOT-DO's. These are the things you want to do, or know that you should do, but yet you don't. You have a subconscious block to taking your best course of action. They include laziness, irresponsibility, writer's block, stage fright, speaker's panic, timidity (for example to approach the opposite sex), resistance to exercise, and all phobias.

HAVE: your Results in the physical universe.

Your NEIRs block your manifesting what you want in life. When you are operating in NEIRs such as: *I am unable; I am a failure; I am the victim; I am undeserving; I am unworthy* etc.; you will manifest affirming events and circumstances.

BEing is SUPREME! You cannot manifest anything that would contradict your creation of your Self, Who You Are. Lesser things than your BEing, your material events (things, people and circumstances) **cannot contradict, violate, WHO YOU ARE** – and that by your own creation (of NEIRs). BEing is supreme in the Creation; all other creations bow before it.

Is a person who is, *by his own creation*, NEIRs such as unable, incapable, weak, a failure, going to be able to manifest notable success? Is a person who is, *by his own creation*, unworthy and undeserving, going to be able to manifest a great relationship or abundant income?

It should be obvious that NO. Life works BE→HAVE. The great error that people make is that they try to live HAVE→BE. They try to accumulate all the external symbols of success so they can then BE-FEEL themselves successful, powerful, respected, etc. It does not work, and **this is living life backwards**: life works BE→HAVE, not HAVE→BE.

The correct way to HAVEing what you want in life is to first discreate your NEIRs that counteract your intelligence, power, and worthiness; then **re-create yourself in PEIRs of BEing smart, wise, capable, and a success**. From such positive states of Self, you will then naturally and easily manifest those things that go with such a BEing. In fact, they will come to you with little effort because the universe supports you BEing Who You Are. The Creation is a field of experience in which each psycan as a child of the Creator, creates and then experiences whatever he wants to. Essence has absolutely no opinion and no objection to whatever you want to create-explore (including to Evil).

You-psycan are in the middle of your creation-exploration of the Human Experience which is primarily Games Conditions, DUPS (and Evil). You change movies to Power, Abundance, and Happiness whenever you want and do the work on Self necessary. The Psycanics Science Institute and the Essentiality School of Accelerated Enlightenment exist to guide you in that work.

In the support sessions for Book III, you will take your actual problems that you want to transform, and be piloted to find and discreate your causal NEIRs, then to re-create your BEing in the PEIRs that naturally manifest your desired results in each Arena. We "hold your hand" while you learn to do it.

25- Essentiality

Physics deals with trans-physical energy, matter, space, time, forces, movements, change, and resistances, all of which produce human experience and behaviors. Psycanics is the physics of trans-physical energy and matter (realities). The supreme force in psycanics is you-psycan; your will, which moves energy, forms realities and can discreate them.

Your trans-physical energies, as we have seen, are those that are beyond the physical universe. They include your emotions, your thoughts, your identities, your motivations and impulses to behaviors, values, relationship energies, likes and aversions, love, and the net result of all the above according to whether they are positive or negative: Happiness<>UPS. They are trans-physical energies because they are not in the physical universe; they come from beyond the physical universe. You can't measure them or capture them with physical instruments. You-psycan experience them directly in your consciousness. They have nothing to do with the FU. When your body dies, you-psycan-consciousness and your psycanic experiences continue. (See reports of NDE on YouTube.)

Psycanics comes from Essentiality. **Essentiality is a science of spirituality** and a system for *real-izing* (making real in your experience) **Who You Really Are: an immortal spirit, child of Essence.**

At the core of all religions there is a legend or myth of some place, state of consciousness, or BEing beyond human perception. ITs names are legion: God, Allah, Tao, Brahma, the Kingdom of Heaven, Garden of Paradise, Enlightenment, Samadhi, Nirvana, Realization, etc. The legends tell that it is the Creator of everything including man; that we are children of IT; IT is our origin and nature ("made in the image and likeness"). The legends state that it is the **supreme value** of life, worth any price. And the legends declare that we can, with right effort, rediscover and return to IT.

To come to Earth and play at being human, you-psycan must block out all the Truth of Nature of Existence (Essence) and Who You Are. You must create "avidya", (ignorance, amnesia, in Buddhism and Hinduism). You must reduce your WPVLJ to negative levels (anti-Essence) to play Games, maintain Game Conditions to explore Drama and UPS. You have done this perfectly! You do not experience Who You Really Are right now; and you have lots of Drama and UPS in your life. You are trapped in avidya and your creation-illusion of being only a human being. Congratulations! That was your plan and you have executed it perfectly. How much more of the human experience, of DUPS, do you want?

You are a free BEing; Essence has no laws, no commandants, no requirements. ABOLUTELY NONE. You are free to stay here in the Human Illusion and explore the negative (painful) side of BEing and of the Creation as long as you wish. You have already been through hundreds of human incarnations. Soon or later, your spirit will tire of the Human Drama, and want to return to Love. You will experience this as the Dark Night of the Old Soul, and it means it is time to start working on yourself to Awaken to Who You Really Are and end your cycle of incarnations in Samsara. (Hinduism, see glossary.) It is not a "salvation" or a "redemption"; there is nothing wrong with you and nothing to save you from. Essence always knows exactly where you are, and She will bring you Home when you commit to traveling. True Spirituality is an Awakening from the Human Dream --Nightmare?-- an En-lighten-ment: the light of understanding the Truth of your existence. It is a Going Home to Essence whence you come.

I can tell you all this because I, and dozens of others in the ESAE (Essentiality School of Accelerated Enlightenment), have awakened. We are living all that we talk about. We speak and teach from personal experience, not from ancient, dead doctrines and dogmas. We have discreated much of our human identity shell and live in the experience of BEing spirits visiting Earth and using a body to maneuver here. We also can perceive and feel Essence, Infinite Love-Joy, all around and within us; and we can communicate with Her.

Having used BTT for some years, we are free of all negative human emotions, of Drama and UPS. We are free of jealousy and envy, of ambition and greed, of the negative ego of believing ourselves better or worse than others. (All UHBs have neg-ego.) We are free of the past, of resentments and all neg-energy from relationships; we are free of sorrows, loneliness, emo-charges about errors or failures. We are free of painful memories and traumatic incidents, of the idea that anybody owes us anything. Our relationships are all harmonious. We are free of the External Quest, of wanting anything material as the mirage of happiness. We live in abundance consciously manifest what we need; and actually, we seldom have to do this: Essence sends us what we need often before we even realize that we need it. We work every day on expanding our spiritual state and achieving ever greater contact with Essence.

There is nothing special about us or about what we achieved: enlightenment and freedom from the world. We are all equal beings. We all come from the same place (Essence) with the same powers. What we have done, anyone can do who is willing to make the effort. Our mission in life is to help those who seek Enlightenment. To that end, we are created a system of study and processes that produce Enlightenment in only 5 years with about 2 hours of disciplines per day.

Who You Are and the ultimate nature of the Creation is one and the same. Ultimate Reality is One Infinite BEing who is the only thing the really exists. This One BEing manifests the Creation out of her own Essence which has the 13 Primordial Characteristics of Oneness/Unity, Infinity, Light, Consciousness, Wisdom, Will (Power), Perfection, Beauty, Magnificence, Love, Peace, Joy, and Truth. You-psycan are an illusory individualization of the One Essence. You individuate from Essence to play in the Creation. Right now, you are playing the Human Game, starring in your Human Movie.

The Human Adventure requires that you go far from Essence, far from Love and Joy, into Darkness and Drama. To play the Human Game, you must not-know Who You Really Are, for which purpose you created *avidya*, the word in Buddhism and Hinduism for spiritual ignorance.

Eventually you will tire of being so far from Love and long to recover your original nature Wisdom, Power, Love, and Joy. Essentiality is a system for doing so. In Essentiality, you do not just discreate a few negative experiences; you must completely clean your BEing of ALL negative energy. This takes the aforementioned 5 years. At the end of the work on your Self, you will transcend the illusion of being only a human being, recover your experience of yourself as an immortal spirit, and be able to perceive and communicate with Essence. This level of consciousness is known in Buddhism and Hinduism as "Enlightenment".

The Essentiality School of Accelerated Enlightenment ESAE

The ESAE (Essentiality School of Accelerated Enlightenment) is exactly that: a school of **mysticism** for spiritual enlightenment and then illumination, the fifth and highest of five levels of consciousness, the level of Buddha and Jesus. Mysticism is the exploration and experience of levels of energy and BEing beyond normal human perception, in particular of the Supreme BEing. The

Essentiality books at www.Essentiality.org explain what True Spirituality is and what human existence really is.

END of BOOK

Thank you for reading this book.

We trust it has been an eye-opener. We hope to see you join those few human beings who want to awaken from the human illusion and commitment to Drama, and recover their Creator Power over their lives.
We are here to support you.

See www.Psycanics.org for how to continue your studies.

See www.Essentiality.org for information about
Essentiality and Spiritual Enlightenment.

Glossary

Abbreviations

aka: also known as, indicating an alternate name or synonym.

CCC: Creation-Counter-Creation: Intent to create positive can activate negatives.

BFTRDH: The Causal Sequence of BE→FEEL→THINK→RELATE & DO→HAVE

DOR: Denial of Responsibility = creation of Victim

ESAE: The Essentiality School for Accelerated Enlightenment.

Exp: Experience

Exp2: Experienced Experience: the fundamental operation of BTT

Exp2→0: Experienced Experience Disappears

ICI: Intention-Counter-Intention

IMHO: In My Humble Opinion, as opposed to Truth which is always verifiable.

MOPs: Moments of Pleasure: activations of PEIRs by external events.

MODs: Moments of Dolor (Pain) activations of NEIR masses.

NEIR: Negative Essence Identity Reality

PECRED: Psycan Energy Creation Reality Experience Discreation

PEIR: Positive Essence Identity Reality

R, Rs: Reality, Realities

Resp: Responsability

RespExp: Responsability for Experience

RELDO: abbreviation for DO & RELATE in the Causal Sequence

RExp: Reality-Experience: two sides of the same coin.

SEB: Spiritually Enlightened Being. Psycans who have transcended the illusion of only being human to recover their consciousness of themselves as immortal spirits and to restore their connection and communication with Essence.

SNB: Should Not Be, the meaning of "bad"

TE: Time and Energy, the substance of your life.

UHB: Unenlightened Human Being. Human beings living in avidya (spiritual ignorance of who they are). They create Drama and explore BEing evil and being done to by evil.

UPS: Unhappiness, Pain, and Suffering. All forms of negative experience in any Arena BFTRDH, especially the negative emotions.

WPVLJ: Wisdom, Power, Value, Love-Joy: the four Characteristics of the 13 Characteristics of Essence that most impact and determine human experience. Their negative polarities are the NEIRs.

Concepts

3 Dimensions of experience: Physical, Psycanic, and Spiritual.

6 Arenas of life: BE, FEEL, THINK, RELATE & DO, HAVE; corresponding to Identities, Emotions, Mind, Relationships, Actions and Behaviors, and material Results

13 Primordial Characteristics: TT Essentiality The ultimate nature of the One Supreme BEing, Creator and Essence of all that is. Her 13 Characteristics are Oneness/Unity, Infinity, Light, Consciousness, Wisdom, Will (Power), Perfection, Beauty, Magnificence, Love, Truth, Joy, Peace.

aka: abbreviation for "**also known as**", indicating an alternate name or synonym.

Aberration: any deviation in experience or behavior from what is desired. Aberrations include: all the negative emotions; all negative behaviors such as addictions, compulsions, obsessions, phobias; and all relationship problems and conflicts; everything that is UPS. Also includes problematic physical results: lack of money, health problems, failures.

Activation. An activation is the triggering and movement of a NEIR mass from your subconscious to your consciousness-experience. You may feel the NEIR mass primarily as negative emotions, but the NEIRs are always there.

Anti-Love, aka neg-love: The south pole of the Love<>Evil Polarity. All forms of negative energy and actions. Essentiality: synonym for Evil.

Arena: any of the 6 areas of experience in life, in the Causal Sequence. In psycanics, they are: BE→FEEL→THINK→RELATE & DO→HAVE. Essentiality adds in the two spiritual dimensions: ESSENCE →PSYCAN→ BE→FEEL→THINK→RELATE & DO→HAVE

BFTDH or BFTRDH: abbreviation for BE→FEEL→THINK→REL-DO→HAVE: The Six Arenas of Experience, which form the Causal Sequence.

Bad: that which Should Not Be (SNB) apparently justifying the use of resistance and negative energy to stop, change, punish or destroy that "bad" entity. (We say apparently because under the Laws of Love, negative energy, negative love, is never justified.) See Bad-SNB.

Bad-SNB: abbreviation for "Bad, Wrong, and therefore Should-Not-Be". Bad-SNB is a hallucination of the human mind. Whenever you label something Bad-SNB, you are saying that thing should not exist. If it exists, it has the approval of Essence (God) to exist: if Her Omnipotence did not want something to exist, it would not. Essence wants everything possible to exist.

Baggage: All the negative energy and acts (neg-love) that the being has accumulated during his life. It includes painful memories, traumatic incidents (violence, abuse, rape, etc.), abandonment, failures, shame, guilt, resentments, relationships ended with negative energy, evil acts to others, theft, deceptions, etc. the Being Transformation Technology cleans baggage from the being. All neg-love acts lower the Love-Light of the being and must be cleaned and the energy restored.

BE: First element of the Causal Sequence.: BE→FEEL→THINK→DO→HAVE

BE-FEEL: 1- noun: The first two elements of the Causal Sequence which are inseparable. Your FEEL (emotions) are your love energy for Self+/- determined by your BE (identities: PEIRs<>NEIRs) of the moment. 2- verb: to open to and integrate with an identity letting yourself BE that identity and so FEEL it, experience it, as Self.

Being: All that you are BEing, also defined by all that you are not BEing. The collection, complex, of identities that the psycan takes on to become a particular entity, person or role. Shells of being are sets of realities that act upon the psycan-consciousness to generate the experience of being a chosen identity. A being is a psycan modulated by his identities, his creations of what he is and is not, thus producing a unique individual. Analogy: In a human movie, the psycan is the actor; his being is his role, his character, in the movie. Where the distinction is not important "psycan" and "being" may be used as a synonym. To become a human being requires 3 Shells of being: evil, drama, and avatar.

Being Transformation Technology: An extensive and sophisticated system of protocols, procedures, and processes that apply the know-how of Psycanics or Essentiality to the psycan enabling him to make desired changes in his being and life. Much of it deals with the creation and discreation of psycanic realities and identities.

Integrally Rich Life: The creation of the realities/experiences that you desire in all of the 12 areas of life. The UHB will create no-results=drama in multiple areas of his life. The SEB manifests what he wants in all areas.

Causal Sequence of Life: The formula of how life works: BE→FEEL→ THINK→RELATE & DO→HAVE, wherein the element to the left determines the elements to the right. The BEing, the leftmost element, is the ultimate causal factor and is the creator of all the other areas. The power of the Causal Sequence is that upon changing your BE that entire Sequence, your life, changes. The avidya UHB struggles to change effects: HAVE, DO, THINK, and FEEL. The SEB goes directly to BE, transforms himself with Being Transformation Technology and all the rest of his Sequence changes automatically.

Cocoon: synonym for the Shell. The Cocoon / Shell is a huge, multi-dimensional mass of ECRE around the psycan that acts upon his consciousness-experience to produce his experience (illusion) of BEing only a human being. It programs for him his unique human identity, including personality and character. It contains his NEIR masses and therefore all his negative emotions. One of the objectives of psycanics is to go out into the Cocoon and discreate negative realities and create positive ones to thereby transform one's experience and behaviors.

Consciousness: One of the 13 Primordial Characteristics of Essence, of Life: to wit, the power to perceive, feel, experience and thereby know energy and realities. It is related to Wisdom and intelligence, intuition and creativity. Consciousness does not come from matter or anywhere in the Creation; it is a priori; it is part of the Creator and therefore basic to the psycan

Cosmos: capital "C". Synonym for the Creation (capital "C"). The entirety of all created realities, all dimensions, all universes. Do not confuse Cosmos in Essentiality with the astronomical definition of the word as the physical universe. Our entire physical universe is no more than a grain of sand in the Cosmos.

Create: To create is to cause into existence something new, something that did not exist before. Creator Will moves energy to form realities out of energy: that is the process of creation. Manifestation is to attract into your experience (life) something already created, usually by others. You create a painting or a business or a relationship. You manifest a car or money or a house. You create by using your will to forming the mental image of the desired result and then energizing (loving) it.

Creator: That which causes something to exist. Capital "C" indicates the word is used as a name for Essence. Essence is the Creator of the Cosmos; the psycan is a creator of his experience and life.

Creation: 1- capital "C": Synonym for the Cosmos meaning all dimensions of the Energy (Essence) with all their universes and all created realities. Everything that exists except the Essence Creator Herself who exists outside or and beyond the Creation as well as existing as the Creation.

creation: 2- small "c": any reality; all realities are creations. Every thought is a creation, every tree is a creation, every human being is a creation, every star is a creation, every universe is a creation. You are the creator of all your realities. Realities produce experience: ergo you are the creator of all your experience, particularly psycanic experience.

Culture-ization, culturization: The teaching and learning (mostly informal and unconscious) of a culture, which consists of a unique set of values, beliefs, programs and paradigms. For example, Japan, USA, Mexico, Germany as examples, all have very different cultures. Cultures must be absorbed by new members, usually the children, as they are growing up. Note that culture is entirely psycanic. If you take a Japanese baby and raise him in Mexico, he will be Mexican. See also socialization.

Dark Night of the Old Soul: TT Essentiality. As the psycan tires of the Human Experience after hundreds of incarnations, he begins to long for Home, for Essence. The Dark Night is the symptoms of this tiring and therefore readiness for Awakening.

Darkside of the Creation: TT Essentiality. All forms of negative energy, experiences and actions, including NEIRs and Evil.

Discreate: To cause a creation, a reality, to no longer exist. This is done by discharging, liberating, the energy that comprises the reality. (The energy is not discreated, it is freed. It ceases to form that reality.) The psycan-consciousness has the power to discreate its creations by experiencing them which is to flow their energy from the reality to consciousness.

DO-BE-DO: The law that what you DO defines, creates, who you are, who you BE. This actually a feedback loop between BE and DO. Example: Steal (DO) and you are a thief (BE). Being a thief, what you DO is steal.

Don Quixote, the Don Quixote Behaviors: All the negative behaviors that humans in the External Quest do to try to control their MODs and UPS, and achieve MOPS, especially those that deal with other people. As nothing in the external world ever causes internal experience, such people are living like Don Quixote hallucinating that windmills (external things) are dragons the cause of MODs).

REL-DO: abbreviation for DO and RELATE in in the Causal Sequence. RELATE is a special case of DO: it is all your actions in relationships, comprising three categories: what you say and how you say it; how you treat and deal with others; and how you either react with MODs or respond with wisdom and love to others' treatment of you.

Drama: TT Psycanics. Drama is all the varied and rich experience, mostly negative, that we savor during a Game (or a movie). Life and everything in life is a Game. Drama includes: effort and struggle, problems, conflicts, uncertainty, doubt, suspense, frustration, impotence, impatience, anxiety, fear, anger, rage, desperation, depression, allies and enemies, losing and winning, victory and defeat, failure, sadness and sorrow, elation and despair, regret, guilt, giving up or perseverance, etc. Notice that Drama comprises all of the negative emotions, and therefore is mostly UPS (unhappiness, pain, and suffering).

Ectropy<>Entropy: Ectropy is Life, Intelligent Cause, acting in the universe to differentiate and control matter, to form it into realities with the desired properties, to organize it and energize it to produce whatever the desired result. Opposite: Entropy

Emotion: The self-love energy polarity. Your emotions are your love<>neg-love for yourself determined by your Essence identity (PEIR or NEIR) of the moment.

Entropy<>Ectropy: Entropy is the opposite of ectropy. Entropy is decay and death. Entropy is the force of decay, disorder, and chaos that acts on matter to reduce it to random distribution and minimum energy.

Ectropy is intelligence acting to create things. Example: How much Intelligent Cause does it require to design an automobile, design the factories to produce them, mine the steel, fabricate the parts, assemble them, energize the result with fuel and electricity, and then maintain it while it transports you? That is ectropy. Then leave that automobile abandoned out in a field for 100 years: the result is a pile of rust. That is entropy. The matter has decayed and deteriorated, no differentiation, and minimum energy state. That is entropy.

ESAE: The Essentiality School for Accelerated Enlightenment.

Essence: The infinitely intelligent spiritual Life Energy BEing that is the only thing that exists and which manifests the Creation and all that exists out of Herself, out of Her own energy. She has 13 main Characteristics: Light, Consciousness, Wisdom, Truth, Infinity, Oneness, Will (Power), Magnificence, Perfection, Beauty, Love, Peace, and Joy

Essentiality is a scientific explanation of Essence to the extent that something divine and mystical can be described in words. It is a science of spirituality with the purpose of guiding a human being to develop his spirituality, to eventually recover his consciousness of himself as an immortal, spiritual being and his perception of and communication with Essence. Psycanics comes from Essentiality.

Event: a very general word meaning any change or movement in reality, whether internal, psycanic reality or external, physical reality. Any occurrence is an event. Anything someone says or does is an event. The arrival of a new thought is an event. An activation is an event. The trigger for an activation is an event. The arrival or departure of someone is an event. See also External Event and Trigger Event.

Excelsior: verb: continual improvement to reach excellence and then impeccability.

Existential Imperative of Existence is: "The ultimate motivation of ALL human behavior is to control one's experience." (This has a formal proof.) You see this in everyday life as the avoidance of pain and the pursuit of pleasure (which is mistaken for happiness). However, the ultimate experience, the only true happiness is your level of BEing, of recuperation of Essence-Love-Joy. The underlying truth and power of the Existential Imperative are that we are all trying to get back to God, to the Infinite Wisdom, Power, Love, Joy whence we come. Thus, the highest statement of the Existential Imperative is: The ultimate motivation of all human behavior is to return to Essence.

Explore, exploration: To enter into any experience to know it and live it fully.

Express, expression. Literally: Ex-press: to push out. To do, perform, act. To manifest a quality or characteristic. To think, do, act, or create, and push the result out into the Creation.

Experimenter: one who does experiments, a scientist.

Experiensor: one who experiences, who perceives and feels. As consciousness you are the experiensor of your identities, thoughts, emotions, and relationships (BE FEEL THINK RELATE)

Experience: the perception of a reality by a being. The effect, impact, of a reality on consciousness. Experience is consciousness at work. Experience may be physical, psycanic, or spiritual, although most humans have very little spiritual experience. Psycanic experience is the perception of psycanic realities it occurs directly in the consciousness of the psycan. Physical experiences are perceptions of the physical universe which are experienced through the five senses of the body. Spiritual experiences are the perception of Self, whether the small Self that is the psycan, or the One Infinite Self that is Essence in any of Her 13 Characteristics.

External Event. Any event, any change or occurrence, in the external, physical reality. The term usually refers to Trigger Events for MODs (or MOPs). See Event and Trigger Event. Internal events are changes in your psycanic energies, in thoughts, emotions, identities. These can also trigger MODs.

External Quest: All efforts to control one's psycanic experience by trying to conform to the external world to one's ideas and programs of how it should be. The purpose of all efforts (the Don Quixote Behaviors) is to avoid the activation of MODs (UPS) and produce MOPs (the mirage of happiness. The External Quest obeys the Existential Imperative, but is an Impossible Dream because: 1- nobody has the power to always control externals in his life; and 2- external events do not cause psycanic experience; they are only trigger events for NEIRs and PEIRs. See also: Fatal Identity Sequence, Impossible Dream, Don Quixote.

Evil: TT Essentiality. Evil is the polar opposite of Love, aka neg-love, anti-love. Evil is all forms of negative energy and actions that are entropic; that harm, damage, cause suffering, or destroy. Evil includes anger, hate, bigotry, division, inequality, injustice, criminality (theft, fraud, corruption, etc.), killing, invasion, war, tyranny, terrorism, genocide, etc. An enormous percentage of all human behavior is expressions of evil.

Essentiality: You are a spirit incarnating in the Human Adventure Movie. Psycanics deals with your human life and experience, and how to control them. Essentiality deals with the nature of Essence, the One Infinite Creator BEing, and your relationship with Her.

Fatal Identity; The creation-identity-reality-experience of any form of negation of Cause, Power, or Responsability: Examples include: I am not cause; I am not creator; I am not powerful; I am not responsable; I am not the creator of my psycanic experience. The Fatal Identity starts the Fatal Identity Sequence

Fatal Identity Sequence: The Fatal identity→Fatal Paradigm→the Impossible Dream of the External Quest→Don Quixote Behaviors.

Fatal Paradigm: Whereas external things cause my experience, I must control my external world to control my experience. The Fatal Paradigm is the creation-reality-experience that: Given my Fatal Identity that I am not the creator of my psycanic experience, external things must be. External things (what others do and say and events and situations in my life) determine how I feel and act. The other people in my relationships are the cause of my problems and conflicts with them, not me. Therefore, I must control external things to control my experience, to stop mods and produce my happiness

FU: abbreviation for the "Fisical Universe", the physical universe where all physical energies and realities exist. (The "P" in physical is used for the PU, the Psycanic Universe.)

Game: the effort and struggle to overcome obstacles to reach goals. A game is the struggle and effort, the dance with the obstacles, not the goal. The purpose of a Game is to test mettle to the limits and so to experience maximum Drama. Life and everything in it is a Game for the psycan.

Game Conditions: all the elements that are necessary to keep a Game going: player, goal, obstacle, and balance of power between player and obstacle.

Guilting: Guilting is an additive to blaming; it is the manipulation of others by trying to make them feel guilty (bad and wrong) for something they did for the purpose of controlling them. The purposes of guilting include to punish the person by making them feel bad (embarrassment or shame) so that they do not do it again, or to get them to make amends (usually by doing something the guilter wants). Guilt thing works hand in hand with programs, which are demands and expectations of how others should BFTDH. Example: Parents program their children with a "laundry list" of how they should be and act (to please the parents, make them happy by giving them a MOP). When the child fails to fulfill one of those expectations; they invalidate him/her; they guilt them by labeling them "bad" son/daughter, ungrateful, insensitive, uncaring, unloving, etc. Such programs are called "hooks" in Psycanics, as in: "Her parents have their hooks well implanted in her." Similar: shaming.

Human Being: A psycan in a Shell of realities that generate the illusion of being a unique human character, operating a physical body on planet Earth.

Human Experience: The total cycle of incarnations of a psycan on Earth, 500+. It can be called the Human Experience, Adventure, Exploration, Game, Drama, Movie, Theater, Novel, Sleep, Dream, Descension, etc. These are all synonyms. The one chosen in any particular sentence can be random, or it can depend on which nuance we wish to reference at the moment.

Identity: Any creation of the psycan about himself thereby self-determining what he is and is not. The most important ones are the NEIRs and the PEIRs.

IMHO: Abbreviation for: in my humble opinion. My job is to report Psycanics and Essentiality as they are. So when I say something that is my opinion, I mark it IMHO so there is no confusion with my personal ideas and points of view and the sciences themselves.

Infinite: really, really, really big, such that limits, if any, have never been found.

Intelligence: the mental ability to evaluate a situation, perceive the obstacles and create a successful plan to overcome them to produce the desired results.

Integrally Rich Life: The 12 areas of an integrally rich life are: spiritual, identities or human being, intellectual, emotional, spouse and family, other relationships (work, leadership), body and health, sex, work/career/business, finances, material possessions, and experiences.

Impossible Dream: a synonym for the External Quest, referring to the aspect that the External Quest is impossible for several motives: 1- external events do not cause psycanic experience; they may trigger MODs but they do not create nor can they discreate NEIR masses which are the true cause of all UPS. 2- Even if events did cause MODs, nobody who has ever lived has had the power to always control external events. The nature of life for everyone is that you win some and you lose some.

Love: One of the 13 Characteristics of Essence. Love is all forms of positive energy that care for, help, and grow the energies (the world) around you. Your love for yourself is your emotions +/-. Your love for others is your actions: how you treat them and the energies you use with them. (For example, anger is neg-love.) Opposites: neg-love, anti-love.

The full understanding of Love is complicated and beyond the scope of a glossary. Most human ideas about love are wrong.

Manifest: To manifest is to attract into your experience (life) something already created, usually by others. To create is to cause into existence something new, something that did not exist before. Examples: You manifest a car or money or a person to love. You create a painting or a business or the relationship with the person you attract.

Manifestation: Whatever is manifested. Synonym for reality and for creation.

Matrix: From the famous 1999 movie series starring Keanu Reeves. Matrix is a synonym for the Creation, for the world as an illusion in which we-psycans are playing.

Mind: There is no such thing as a mind. There is the being, aware-will, and his mental realities: thoughts, memories, desires, plans, goals, programs, paradigms, beliefs, religion, values, etc. The being uses his will to create his mental realities, his subconscious to store them out of sight and his consciousness to experience them. We use the term "mind" to refer to mental realities and the processes of creating and experiencing them.

MODs: abbreviation for Moments of Dolor (Latin for pain). MODs are activations of NEIR masses with their negative emotions. MODs are periods of UPS. Synonym: activation.

MOPs: abbreviation for Moments Of Pleasure. MOPs are fleeting activations of positive BE-FEEL (ids→emo) you experience whenever something positive occurs in your life, for example, a vacation, winning a game, etc.). As they require positive external events to trigger them, and events always change; they are not True Happiness: life is ALWAYS a mixture of positive and negative events. If you live making how you FEEL dependent on externals, you will live mostly unhappy.

Movie: A story built around a game which is the struggle to overcome obstacles.

Mu: There are three classifications of realities as regards their truth. Those which are verified and we can be reasonably certain they are the truth. Those which are verified to be false. And all others where the truth of the matter is not verified, and therefore is not known. The label "truth" is the certification of the quality and reliability of the information. It may not be assigned to any datum not verifiable. Those statements are MU. Thus, there are three classifications for information: true, false, and mu. (Example: All advertising that claims to be the best product.

All religions. Political philosophies. Fake news.) Most of what people say and believe is unsubstantiated and therefore mu.

Negative: that which is unpleasant, painful, undesired, counter-productive, harmful, or destructive. All that is entropic: decreases usable energy and increases disorder and chaos, or homogeneity. Negative is NOT Bad-SNB! By the Laws of Polarity, negatives must exist for positives to exist, and they are valid experiences in themselves.

Neg-ego: The hallucination that one person (or group) is superior, greater, or more than another; who is perforce inferior, lesser, worse. This is, obviously, polarization. Neg-ego then polarizes even further into good<>bad, and then hallucinates justification for evil, the use of neg-energy to dominate, conquer, rob, enslave, torture, kill, etc. Both sides of the polarization are neg-ego; it is equally neg-ego to hallucinate that you are inferior, less than, worse than others. Neg-ego of superior is an attempt to compensate NEIRs. Neg-inferior comes directly from NEIRs. Neg-ego is part of the Darkside and greatest in Evil. Neg-ego is a hallucination because the Truth is One. There are not two in the One; impossible to have greater or lesser when there is only One. All neg-ego must be discreated for enlightenment. The polar opposite of neg-ego is One and Unity, arrived at by the ascension of the Unity<>Ego Polarity through Humility. Humility comes from the recognition that we are all One; that there can be no greater or lesser. The discreation of NEIRs is also important to achieve Humility.

Neg-emo: abbreviation for "negative emotions". The negative emotions include: anger, rage, hostility, anxiety, fear, terror, horror, resentment, guilt, sadness, sorrow, grief, hate, depression, envy, jealousy, apathy, etc.

Neg-energy: Abbreviation of negative energy which is to say negative love, darkness, evil.

Neg-love: Abbreviation of negative love; all forms of negative energy and negative actions, those that harm others or the Greater Good.

Negative<>Positive: abbreviation for the Positive<>Negative Polarity, which applies to many polarities such as the positive and negative emotions.

NEIRs: abbreviation for Negative Essence Identity Reality. All identities which counter-act Essence, WPVLJ. NEIRs are the polar opposites of PEIRs. See chapter PEIRs<>NEIRs.

Pain: all unpleasant and undesired experience, consisting primarily of negative FEEL, the negative emotions. Pain is the "P" in UPS. In psycanics, "pain" and "suffering" always refer to negative psycanic experience unless physical pain or physical suffering is specified.

Pain and suffering: In Psycanics and Essentiality, "pain" and "suffering" always refer to negative mental and emotional experiences, not physical pain unless "physical" is specified.

PECRED: PECRED is the full sequence of elements of Creation-Experience-Discreation: PECRED is the abbreviation for:

Psycan → Energy → Creation → Reality → Experience → Discreation. This is to be read and understood as: The Psycan (Creator) takes Energy and Creates his Realities, which then cause his Experiences, which then Discreate (on being fully experienced).

PEIR: abbreviation for Positive Essence Identity Reality. See chapter PEIRs<>NEIRS

PEIRs<>NEIRs: Positive Essence Identity Realities <> Negative Essence Identity Realities. PEIRs affirm the 4 characteristics of Essence of Wisdom, Power, Value, and Goodness (Love). NEIRs deny or counter-create them. PEIRs and NEIRs form the BE in the Causal Sequence. There are four great NEIR masses in the Shell.

Pilot, piloting: A person highly trained in Being Transformation Technology and in how to guide others. All teachers of Psycanics and Essentiality must first be pilots.

Polarity: The "stretching" of any type of experience into a spectrum of gradients between two opposing poles. It is impossible to understand existence without understanding the laws of polarity.

Polarize, Polarization: To divide people or groups and label one side superior<>inferior, which progresses to good<>bad, apparently justifying neg-love (evil) to the "bad" side. The anti-love to the "bad" side can include: invalidation, judgments, criticisms, rejection, ostracism, punish, and even death. Examples can be seen in racism, nationalism, religions, politics.

Positive: that which is pleasant, desired, constructive, productive, useful. All that is ectropic; all that increases the organization and energy state of a system (which requires intelligent Cause).

Positive<>Negative: the Positive<>Negative Polarity. See definitions of positive and negative.

Power: The ability to produce the desired results in any area of life, and particularly to create and discreate. Your ability to create and live the life you want, to control your destiny.

Process: Any of a myriad of ways of moving energy, creating and discreating realities to make changes in your BEing and therefore in your Causal Sequences= your life. A process may follow formal protocols, or a good pilot can invent one on the spot to guide his explorer to achieve his desired result. BTT has hundreds of processes. Processes have protocols.

Protocol: A protocol is all the formal, written instructions, rules and procedures to be followed to produce a particular result. In BTT, a protocol is the procedures and steps of standard flows of questions and instructions for creation and discreation during sessions of BTT.

Psycanics: Psycanics is the physics of trans-physical human energies and experience. It models the workings of the emotions, the mind, the being, behaviors, relationships, love◇anti-love, and happiness◇UPS. Psycanics describes their operations with exact laws, principles and formulas. It is a psychology of human experience and behavior that is derived from Essentiality. One of the applications of psycanics is the Being Transformation Technology, a very powerful form of psychotherapy. Psycanics deals with realities that every human being experiences all the time, as contrasted with Essentiality which deals with spiritual experiences that require preparation and practice to perceive. Psycanics is a trickle-down of Essentiality.

Psycanic, psycanic experience: Psycanic means pertaining to the psycan. Psycanics experience is all realities-experience that the psycan perceives directly in consciousness as opposed to physical realities that he perceives through the instrument of his body. Psycanic experience includes BE, FEEL, THINK, and RELATE: identities, emotions, thoughts, and relationship energies with others.

PU: abbreviation for "Psycanic Universe", the trans-physical space around the psycan wherein he creates all his psycanic ECRE: thoughts, emotions, identities, and where the Shell exists.

Real: The condition of a reality when it is being experienced. A reality not being experienced is not-real. Not-real does not mean that it does not exist, only that it is out of perception. Most of the Shell is not-real most of the time.

Reality: Any mass or form of energy with its own identity, differentiating it from all other forms of energy. If it exists it is a reality. A reality is "energy with an identity"; it is energy being some particular thing, object, or experience. Psycanic realities include identities, NEIRs, PEIRs, emotions, and all thought-forms. Realities cause experience. PECRED is the laws of reality, there creation and discreation.

Reality versus Truth: Every idea is a psycanic reality. Truth exists only when a statement (a psycanic reality) is verified as corresponding to the reality it is describing. Where there is no verification, the truth is not known and it is a lie to call that reality "truth" when it is mu. Understanding this is very important in relationships.

RExp: pronounced "rex". Reality and Experience are the two sides of the same coin. Realities cause experience; experience is the effect of a reality on consciousness.

Responsability: TT with a cap "R" and an "a": 1- Ability to respond, to take action. 2- Recognition of Cause followed by action. 3- A personal decision that ends victim.

Responsibility: Not a TT and with an "i": A duty to care for or do something, or produce a certain result. A legal or moral obligation.

Resistance: First level: negation to experience through avoidance or suppression of the experience often with addictive substances or activities. Second level: any use of negative energy of any kind to attack, change, stop, punish or destroy the negative experience, and or its triggers.

Samsara: Buddhism and Hinduism: Life on earth is Samsara. It includes 3 concepts:

1- The long cycle of many human incarnations. The entire cycle of our descent from Essence to the Human Experience consists of 500 to 700 human incarnations.

2 - Pain and suffering. In the ultimate analysis, human existence is more pain and suffering than enjoyment and happiness for multiple reasons:

3- Trapped. We are locked into samsara, reincarnation after reincarnation, by the our Darkside identity mass. This identity mass traps us on earth until we discreate it. What the Anti-Essence Identity is and how it works is the subject of Advanced Essentiality.

SEB: TT Essentiality. Abbreviation for a Spiritually Enlightened Being: A psycan who has awakened from the Human Dream, recovered his self-experience of immortal spiritual BEing. He has perception and communication with Essence and can feel the Oneness of all that is. He is a Master of Life creating his human existence as he wants it. He is free of the External Quest, negative emotions, of Game Conditions and Drama, of the past and of the future, and of relationship problems. He lives in serenity and joy and uses his restored creator power to manifest what he wants in life.

Self: Synonym for the BEing. My Self = my BEing.

Shell: the Shell is a cloud of energy and realities around the psycan that acts upon his consciousness to create the illusion of human being. In the Shell is programmed personality, characters, likes and dislikes and all non-physical experience and behaviors. Synonym: Cocoon.

Sleep: Synonym for avidya, for not knowing Who You Are and so being lost in the Human Dream.

Socialization: the teaching and learning (mostly informal and unconscious) of how to get along with others in family, groups and society; of manners, ways of speaking, and behaviors that avoid frictions and conflicts with others. Example of socialization: respecting the property of others. Without socialization, we would behave like animals. Socialization is related to culturization but not the same thing

SNB: abbreviation for Should Not Be, the basic opinion and reality constituent of the Hallucination of Bad-SNB. The prime characteristic of anything bad is that it should not exist. It is a hallucination because the Truth of the Creation is that there is nothing that should not be: the Purpose of the Creation is ALL experiences possible.

Space: The absence of all energy, especially negative energy. The neutral, midway point on the Energy Polarity (Love Polarity) between positive and negative. It is therefore the end of anti-love and the beginning of love. Related concept: Transparency.

Spirituality: Your degree of experience and expression of Essence in Her 13 Characteristics. The characteristics of spirituality include Wisdom, Power, Love, Responsability, Humility, Transparency, Service, Discipline, Excellence, Integrity. To find a School, you need a true source of spirituality. You must be clear on how to identify a True Source; there are many more scammers, false prophets, and ineffective schools on the planet than there are True Sources.

Subconscious: The psycanic space around the psycan but outside of his conscious perception. Synonym: the unconscious.

Suffering: Suffering is resistance to pain, to negative experience, which intensifies and persists it. (Laws of Energy: Resistance Causes Pain and Persistence.) Suffering is any intense and long-lasting negative emotional state (anger, fear, hate, sorrow, depression, etc.). Suffering is pain about pain. Your negative emotions are unpleasant, painful, but they are not suffering. Suffering is resistance to negative experience, to pain. You turn pain into suffering by resisting your negative experience. You are the sole creator of all your suffering in life. Nothing external to you is ever the cause of your suffering.

TE: abbreviation for Time & Energy. In the ultimate analysis, the only thing that you have in life is your Time and your Energy. Your life is your TE. There are many forms of energy: work, money, design and planning, food, gasoline, transportation, and all other things. You can interchange energy (e.g. giving food)) for time, or your time (e.g. work) for energy (money).

Transparency: The absence of negative energy and resistance. A state of being that is non-reactive and non-resistant to others and events. 2- On the Love Energy Polarity, Transparency is the point of no or neutral energy between Love and Evil.

Trigger, trigger event. Any occurrence, any change or movement of any energy which sets off an activation, a MOD. A trigger event can be psycanic, such as one's own thoughts; or it can be external, physical such as something that someone says or does, or something that happens in the life of the person. See Event, External Event

Truth: The verified or verifiable correspondence between a reality and a statement about that reality. Where there is no verification, the truth is not known and may not be claimed honestly. "Truth" is a certification of the "quality" of a statement. Humans confuse their mental realities (beliefs) with truth.

Two Paths: There are a number of "Two Paths" in psycanics and Essentiality. In this book, there are mentioned:

1. Responsability <> Victim

2. Results <> Drama

3. Discreation of Realities <> Resistance-Persistence to Experience

4. Discreate NEIRs when activated<>Keep your MODs all your life.

UHB- TT Essentiality. Abbreviation for Unenlightened Human Being. The, ordinary human being in avidya, asleep to Essence and Who He Really Is, lost in his human identity, and living in Game Conditions and DUPS.

Universal Principles: The Principles of treating others with Love. The Principles include: Integrity (honesty, sincerity), punctuality, keeping your word, and Space to the other. When ET shows up, we will treat him according to the Universal Principles, or there will be problems.

UPS: abbreviation for **unhappiness, pain, and suffering**, which are always psycanic in nature in Psycanics unless physical pain or physical suffering is specified. UPS comprises all forms of negative emotions, thoughts, and identities.

Victim: a person who denies all incumbency and responsability for her experience, whether that is what happens to her in the physical universe, or her negative emotions, or her relationship problems, or anything else in her life. A Victim assigns Cause to external agents thereby creating herself as Effect and therefore powerless. The major characteristic of a Victim is DOR: Denial of Responsability. "Victim" is the polar opposite of Power and Creator.

Who You Really Are: There are two levels to your Being: 1- your spirit-ual individuality as an entity of Aware-Will: psycan. 2- Beyond the illusion of individuality: the One Infinite Essence that we all are. You are Essence, then One. Your psycan-individuality is an illusion so that you can descend into and play in the Creation.

Will: One of the 13 Characteristics of Essence; the power to move and form energy, thereby to create realities.

WPVLJ (pronounced Whipple) abbreviation for: Wisdom, Power, Value, Love-Joy, the 4 of the 13 characteristics of Essence that dominate human experience and behavior. Affirmations of WPVLJ are the PEIRs; counter creations to WPVLJ are the NEIRs,

Wisdom: The ability to predict consequences of actions and so to avoid negative experiences and results and produce positive ones.

Yin and Yang: Yin<>Yang is one of the fundamental polarities of the Creation. Yin is the feminine element: receptive, passive, patient, softness, shadow, coolness, relaxedness, perceptive, intuitive, enjoyment, present time, flowing, malleable, adjustable. Yang is the masculine element: force, power, action, productivity, rational, logical, future time, rigid, light, heat. Essence is both yin and yang, but Her nature is more yin. Male-female relationships work best when they are highly polarized in yin and yang. The negative polarity of yang is neg-ego, aggression and force, damage and destruction. The negative polarity of yin is irrationalism, flightiness, no reliability, does not respect word and promises, disorganization and chaos.